TRANSIT COOPERATIVE RESEARCH PROGRAM

TCRP REPORT 95

Traveler Response to Transportation System Changes
Chapter 13—Parking Pricing and Fees

ERIN VACA
and
J. RICHARD KUZMYAK
Lead Chapter Authors

RICHARD H. PRATT, CONSULTANT, INC.
Garrett Park, MD

TEXAS TRANSPORTATION INSTITUTE
College Station, TX

JAY EVANS CONSULTING LLC
Washington, DC

PARSONS BRINCKERHOFF QUADE & DOUGLAS, INC.
Baltimore, MD and San Francisco, CA

CAMBRIDGE SYSTEMATICS, INC.
Chevy Chase, MD

J. RICHARD KUZMYAK, L.L.C.
Silver Spring, MD

BMI-SG
Vienna, VA

GALLOP CORPORATION
Rockville, MD

McCOLLOM MANAGEMENT CONSULTING, INC.
Darnestown, MD

HERBERT S. LEVINSON, TRANSPORTATION CONSULTANT
New Haven, CT

K.T. ANALYTICS, INC.
Bethesda, MD

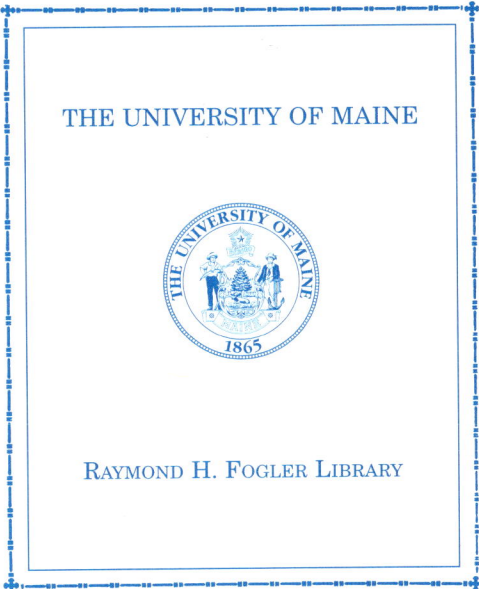

SUBJECT AREAS
Planning and Administration • Public Transit • Highway Operations, Capacity and Traffic Control

Research Sponsored by the Federal Transit Administration in Cooperation with the Transit Development Corporation

TRANSPORTATION RESEARCH BOARD

WASHINGTON, D.C.
2005
www.TRB.org

The nation's growth and the need to meet mobility, environmental, and energy objectives place demands on public transit systems. Current systems, some of which are old and in need of upgrading, must expand service area, increase service frequency, and improve efficiency to serve these demands. Research is necessary to solve operating problems, to adapt appropriate new technologies from other industries, and to introduce innovations into the transit industry. The Transit Cooperative Research Program (TCRP) serves as one of the principal means by which the transit industry can develop innovative near-term solutions to meet demands placed on it.

The need for TCRP was originally identified in *TRB Special Report 213—Research for Public Transit: New Directions,* published in 1987 and based on a study sponsored by the Urban Mass Transportation Administration—now the Federal Transit Administration (FTA). A report by the American Public Transportation Association (APTA), *Transportation 2000,* also recognized the need for local, problem-solving research. TCRP, modeled after the longstanding and successful National Cooperative Highway Research Program, undertakes research and other technical activities in response to the needs of transit service providers. The scope of TCRP includes a variety of transit research fields including planning, service configuration, equipment, facilities, operations, human resources, maintenance, policy, and administrative practices.

TCRP was established under FTA sponsorship in July 1992. Proposed by the U.S. Department of Transportation, TCRP was authorized as part of the Intermodal Surface Transportation Efficiency Act of 1991 (ISTEA). On May 13, 1992, a memorandum agreement outlining TCRP operating procedures was executed by the three cooperating organizations: FTA; the National Academies, acting through the Transportation Research Board (TRB); and the Transit Development Corporation, Inc. (TDC), a nonprofit educational and research organization established by APTA. TDC is responsible for forming the independent governing board, designated as the TCRP Oversight and Project Selection (TOPS) Committee.

Research problem statements for TCRP are solicited periodically but may be submitted to TRB by anyone at any time. It is the responsibility of the TOPS Committee to formulate the research program by identifying the highest priority projects. As part of the evaluation, the TOPS Committee defines funding levels and expected products.

Once selected, each project is assigned to an expert panel, appointed by the Transportation Research Board. The panels prepare project statements (requests for proposals), select contractors, and provide technical guidance and counsel throughout the life of the project. The process for developing research problem statements and selecting research agencies has been used by TRB in managing cooperative research programs since 1962. As in other TRB activities, TCRP project panels serve voluntarily without compensation.

Because research cannot have the desired impact if products fail to reach the intended audience, special emphasis is placed on disseminating TCRP results to the intended end users of the research: transit agencies, service providers, and suppliers. TRB provides a series of research reports, syntheses of transit practice, and other supporting material developed by TCRP research. APTA will arrange for workshops, training aids, field visits, and other activities to ensure that results are implemented by urban and rural transit industry practitioners.

The TCRP provides a forum where transit agencies can cooperatively address common operational problems. The TCRP results support and complement other ongoing transit research and training programs.

Project B-12A FY'99
ISSN 1073-4872
ISBN 0-309-08763-5
Library of Congress Control Number 2003108813

© 2005 Transportation Research Board

Price $20.00

Published reports of the

TRANSIT COOPERATIVE RESEARCH PROGRAM

are available from:

Transportation Research Board
Business Office
500 Fifth Street, NW
Washington, DC 20001

and can be ordered through the Internet at
http://www.national-academies.org/trb/bookstore

Printed in the United States of America

THE NATIONAL ACADEMIES
Advisers to the Nation on Science, Engineering, and Medicine

FOREWORD

By Stephan A. Parker
Staff Officer
Transportation Research
Board

This "Parking Pricing and Fees" chapter addresses traveler response to both the introduction of parking pricing and fees and to changes in the level, structure, or method of application of parking fees. Included are actions that can change the costs to users of parking even without fee changes, notably through eliminations of employer parking subsidies and by fee structures that differentiate by modes of parking (short/long term) or travel (drive-alone/ridesharing).

Effects of parking pricing are often hard to separate from those of parking supply, while application of parking pricing is frequently accompanied by various other strategies. Thus, there is considerable overlap between this chapter and others. Chapter 18, "Parking Management and Supply," and Chapter 19, "Employer and Institutional TDM Strategies," should be consulted in particular. Effects of parking pricing are felt, and identified where possible, in traveler responses reported for multimodal strategies (Chapters 2 and 3), transit strategies (most importantly Chapters 4, 7, 8, 9, 10 and 12), and land use alternatives (Chapters 15 and 17).

TCRP Report 95: Chapter 13, Parking Pricing and Fees will be of interest to transit, transportation, and land use planning practitioners; educators and researchers; and professionals across a broad spectrum of transportation and planning agencies, MPOs, and local, state, and federal government agencies.

The overarching objective of the *Traveler Response to Transportation System Changes Handbook* is to equip members of the transportation profession with a comprehensive, readily accessible, interpretive documentation of results and experience obtained across the United States and elsewhere from (1) different types of transportation system changes and policy actions and (2) alternative land use and site development design approaches. While the focus is on contemporary observations and assessments of traveler responses as expressed in travel demand changes, the presentation is seasoned with earlier experiences and findings to identify trends or stability, and to fill information gaps that would otherwise exist. Comprehensive referencing of additional reference materials is provided to facilitate and encourage in-depth exploration of topics of interest. Travel demand and related impacts are expressed using such measures as usage of transportation facilities and services, before-and-after market shares and percentage changes, and elasticity.

The findings in the *Handbook* are intended to aid—as a general guide—in preliminary screening activities and quick turn-around assessments. The *Handbook* is not intended for use as a substitute for regional or project-specific travel demand evaluations and model applications, or other independent surveys and analyses.

The Second Edition of the handbook *Traveler Response to Transportation System Changes* was published by USDOT in July 1981, and it has been a valuable tool for transportation professionals, providing documentation of results from different types of transportation actions. This Third Edition of the *Handbook* covers 18 topic areas, including essentially all of the nine topic areas in the 1981 edition, modified slightly in scope, plus nine new topic areas. Each topic is published as a chapter of *TCRP Report 95*. To access the chapters, select "TCRP, All Projects, B-12A" from the TCRP website: http://www.trb.org/tcrp.

A team led by Richard H. Pratt, Consultant, Inc. is responsible for the *Traveler Response to Transportation System Changes Handbook, Third Edition*, through work conducted under TCRP Projects B-12, B-12A, and B-12B.

REPORT ORGANIZATION

The *Handbook*, organized for simultaneous print and electronic chapter-by-chapter publication, treats each chapter essentially as a stand-alone document. Each chapter includes text and self-contained references and sources on that topic. For example, the references cited in the text of Chapter 6, "Demand Responsive/ADA," refer to the Reference List at the end of that chapter. The *Handbook* user should, however, be conversant with the background and guidance provided in *TCRP Report 95: Chapter 1, Introduction*.

Upon completion of the *Report 95* series, the final Chapter 1 publication will include a CD-ROM of all 19 chapters. The complete outline of chapters is provided below.

Handbook Outline Showing Publication and Source-Data-Cutoff Dates

General Sections and Topic Area Chapters (TCRP Report 95 Nomenclature)	U.S. DOT Publication		TCRP Report 95	
	First Edition	Second Edition	Source Data Cutoff Date	Publication Date
Ch. 1 – Introduction (with Appendices A, B)	1977	1981	2003[a]	2000/03/05[a]
Multimodal/Intermodal Facilities				
Ch. 2 – HOV Facilities	1977	1981	1999–05[f]	2000/05[b]
Ch. 3 – Park-and-Ride/Pool	—	1981	2003[c]	2004
Transit Facilities and Services				
Ch. 4 – Busways, BRT and Express Bus	1977[e]	1981	2004[c]	2005[d]
Ch. 5 – Vanpools and Buspools	1977	1981	1999–04[f]	2000/05[b]
Ch. 6 – Demand Responsive/ADA	—	—	1999	2004
Ch. 7 – Light Rail Transit	—	—	2005	2005[d]
Ch. 8 – Commuter Rail	—	—	2005	2005[d]
Public Transit Operations				
Ch. 9 – Transit Scheduling and Frequency	1977	1981	1999	2004
Ch. 10 – Bus Routing and Coverage	1977	1981	1999	2004
Ch. 11 – Transit Information and Promotion	1977	1981	2002	2003
Transportation Pricing				
Ch. 12 – Transit Pricing and Fares	1977	1981	1999	2004
Ch. 13 – Parking Pricing and Fees	1977[e]	—	1999	2000/05[b]
Ch. 14 – Road Value Pricing	1977[e]	—	2002–03[f]	2003
Land Use and Non-Motorized Travel				
Ch. 15 – Land Use and Site Design	—	—	2001–02[f]	2003
Ch. 16 – Pedestrian and Bicycle Facilities	—	—	2004	2005[d]
Ch. 17 – Transit Oriented Design	—	—	2004[d]	2005[d]
Transportation Demand Management				
Ch. 18 – Parking Management and Supply	—	—	2000–02[f]	2003
Ch. 19 – Employer and Institutional TDM Strategies	1977[e]	1981[e]	2005	2005[d]

NOTES: [a] Published in TCRP Web Document 12, *Interim Handbook* (March 2000), without Appendix B. The "Interim Introduction," published in Research Results Digest 61 (September 2003), is a replacement, available at http://www4.trb.org/trb/crp.nsf/All+Projects/ TCRP+B-12A,+Phase+II. Publication of the final version of Chapter 1, "Introduction," as part of the TCRP Report 95 series, is anticipated for 2005.

[b] Published in TCRP Web Document 12, *Interim Handbook*, in March 2000. Available now at http://www4.nas.edu/trb/crp.nsf/ All+Projects/TCRP+B-12. Publication as part of the TCRP Report 95 series is anticipated in 2004 or 2005.

[c] The source data cutoff date for certain components of this chapter was 1999.

[d] Estimated.

[e] The edition in question addressed only certain aspects of later edition topical coverage.

[f] Primary cutoff was first year listed, but with selected information from second year listed.

CHAPTER 13 AUTHOR AND CONTRIBUTOR ACKNOWLEDGMENTS

TCRP Report 95, in essence the Third Edition of the "Traveler Response to Transportation System Changes" Handbook, is being prepared under Transit Cooperative Research Program Projects B-12, B-12A, and B-12B by Richard H. Pratt, Consultant, Inc. in association with the Texas Transportation Institute; Jay Evans Consulting LLC; Parsons Brinckerhoff Quade & Douglas, Inc.; Cambridge Systematics, Inc.; J. Richard Kuzmyak, L.L.C.; BMI-SG; Gallop Corporation; McCollom Management Consulting, Inc.; Herbert S. Levinson, Transportation Consultant; and K.T. Analytics, Inc.

Richard H. Pratt is the Principal Investigator. Dr. Katherine F. Turnbull of the Texas Transportation Institute assisted as co-Principal Investigator during initial Project B-12 phases, leading up to the Phase I Interim Report and the Phase II Draft Interim Handbook. With the addition of Project B-12B research, John E. (Jay) Evans, IV, of Jay Evans Consulting LLC was appointed the co-Principal Investigator. Lead Handbook chapter authors and co-authors, in addition to Mr. Pratt, are Mr. Evans (initially with Parsons Brinckerhoff); Dr. Turnbull; Frank Spielberg of BMI-SG; Brian E. McCollom of McCollom Management Consulting, Inc.; Erin Vaca of Cambridge Systematics, Inc.; J. Richard Kuzmyak, initially of Cambridge Systematics and now of J. Richard Kuzmyak, L.L.C.; and Dr. G. Bruce Douglas, Parsons Brinckerhoff Quade & Douglas, Inc. Contributing authors include Herbert S. Levinson, Transportation Consultant; Dr. Kiran U. Bhatt, K.T. Analytics, Inc.; Shawn M. Turner, Texas Transportation Institute; Dr. Rachel Weinberger, Cambridge Systematics (now with the University of Pennsylvania); Andrew Stryker of Parsons Brinckerhoff; and Dr. C. Y. Jeng, Gallop Corporation.

Other research agency team members contributing to the preparatory research, synthesis of information, and development of this Handbook have been Stephen Farnsworth, Laura Higgins and Rachel Donovan of the Texas Transportation Institute; Nick Vlahos, Vicki Ruiter and Karen Higgins of Cambridge Systematics, Inc.; Lydia Wong, Gordon Schultz, Bill Davidson, and G.B. Arrington of Parsons Brinckerhoff Quade & Douglas, Inc.; Kris Jagarapu of BMI-SG; and Laura C. (Peggy) Pratt of Richard H. Pratt, Consultant, Inc. As Principal Investigator, Mr. Pratt has participated iteratively and substantively in the development of each chapter. Dr. C. Y. Jeng of Gallop Corporation has provided pre-publication numerical quality control review. By special arrangement, Dr. Daniel B. Rathbone of The Urban Transportation Monitor searched past issues. Assistance in word processing, graphics, and other essential support has been provided by Bonnie Duke and Pam Rowe of the Texas Transportation Institute, Karen Applegate, Laura Reseigh, Stephen Bozik, and Jeff Waclawski of Parsons Brincker-hoff, others too numerous to name but fully appreciated, and lastly the warmly remembered late Susan Spielberg of SG Associates (now BMI-SG).

Special thanks go to all involved for supporting the cooperative process adopted for topic area chapter development. Members of the TCRP Project B-12/B-12A/B-12B Project Panel, named elsewhere, are providing review and comments for what will total over 20 individual publication documents/chapters. They have gone the extra mile in providing support on call including leads, reports, documentation, advice, and direction over what will be the eight-year duration of the project. Four consecutive appointed or acting TCRP Senior Program Officers have given their support: Stephanie N. Robinson, who took the project through scope development and contract negotiation; Stephen J. Andrle, who led the work during the Project B-12 Phase and on into the TCRP B-12A Project Continuation; Harvey Berlin, who saw the Interim Handbook through to Website publication; and Stephan A. Parker, who is guiding the entire project to its complete fruition. Editor Natassja Linzau is providing her careful examination and fine touch, while Managing Editor Eileen Delaney and her team are handling all the numerous publication details. The efforts of all are greatly appreciated.

Continued recognition is due to the participants in the development of the First and Second Editions, key elements of which are retained. Co-authors to Mr. Pratt were Neil J. Pedersen and Joseph J. Mather for the First Edition, and John N. Copple for the Second Edition. Crucial support and guidance for both editions was provided by the Federal Highway Administration's Technical Representative (COTR), Louise E. Skinner.

In the *TCRP Report 95* edition, Erin Vaca and J. Richard Kuzmyak are the lead authors for this volume: Chapter 13, "Parking Pricing and Fees."

Participation by the profession at large has been absolutely essential to the development of the Handbook and this chapter. Members of volunteer Review Groups, established for each chapter, reviewed outlines, provided leads, and in many cases undertook substantive reviews. Though all members who assisted are not listed here in the interests of brevity, their contribution is truly valued. Those who have undertaken reviews of Chapter 13 are Andrew Farkas and Peter Valk. In the case of Chapter 13, William G. Allen, Jr., stepped in to provide an independent outside review.

Finally, sincere thanks are due to the many practitioners and researchers who were contacted for information and unstintingly supplied both that and all manner of statistics, data compilations and reports. Though not feasible to list here, many appear in the "References" section entries of this and other chapters.

CHAPTER 13—PARKING PRICING AND FEES

CONTENTS

13 — Parking Pricing and Fees

OVERVIEW AND SUMMARY

This chapter presents information on how travelers respond to both the introduction of parking pricing and fees, and to changes in the level, structure, or method of application of parking fees. Included are actions that can change the costs to users of parking even without fee changes, notably through elimination of employer parking subsidies, and fee structures that differentiate by mode of parking (short/long term) or travel (drive-alone/ridesharing).

Within this "Overview and Summary" section:

- "Objectives of Parking Pricing and Fees" provides an overview of why parking fees might be used as a transportation strategy and what objectives they would serve.

- "Types of Parking Pricing Strategies" outlines the range of parking pricing strategies that have been attempted and identifies which ones are covered in the chapter.

- "Analytical Considerations" highlights the research limitations and caveats of concern when using the traveler response data in the chapter.

- "Traveler Response Summary" encapsulates the key travel demand findings related to parking pricing and fees. It's recommended that all "Overview and Summary" sections be read as background for the "Traveler Response Summary" and the chapter as a whole.

The sections following the "Overview and Summary" are as follows:

- "Response by Type of Strategy" provides greater depth and detail on the travel demand effects of each specific parking pricing strategy quantified as elasticities, modal shares and shifts, and changes in parking behavior.

- "Underlying Traveler Response Factors" explores the interrelationships between parking pricing outcomes and various influences including demographics and land use, travel options and incentives, and behavioral mechanisms.

- "Related Information and Impacts" examines mode and destination shifts, cost effectiveness, and environmental issues and outcomes.

- "Case Studies" presents four comprehensive examples of parking pricing applications.

Effects of parking pricing are often hard to separate from those of parking supply. Moreover, application of parking pricing is frequently accompanied by various other strategies. There is thus considerable overlap between this chapter and others. Chapter 18, "Parking Management and Supply," and Chapter 19, "Employer and Institutional TDM Strategies," should be consulted in particular. Effects of parking pricing are felt, and identified where possible, in traveler responses and related findings reported for multimodal/intermodal applications (Chapters 2 and 3),transit strategies (most importantly Chapters 4, 7, 8, 9, 10, and 12) and land use alternatives (Chapters 15 and 17).

Objectives of Parking Pricing and Fees

The primary objective of setting a price on parking, for parking facility owners/operators, is to cover costs and earn a reasonable return on investment. However, this objective must often be balanced against other objectives, such as the desire to attract shoppers or employees. Prices are also influenced by competition in the private market based on the law of supply and demand, and may also be manipulated by public agencies to realize public policy objectives. Thus, alteration of the level or distribution of parking prices can have many objectives. Among these are:

- Passing along the actual [market] cost of parking from provider to user.
- Differentiating prices among different users to achieve economic, strategic, or policy objectives.
- Reducing the incidence of private vehicle trips, vehicle miles of travel (VMT), and the need for parking spaces associated with private vehicle travel.

The price of parking may be used to influence travel choice by altering the cost of private vehicle travel, and hence its attractiveness, relative to travel alternatives including transit. Effective implementation of parking pricing requires careful consideration of the underlying policy objectives. Parking pricing strategies to reduce VMT may be different from those intended to promote transit use, for example.

Economists suggest that the optimum parking fee per unit time should be set equal to the marginal cost of providing a parking space, since parking cost and availability are closely tied to vehicle usage and roadway congestion. Parking fees have been suggested as an alternative to roadway pricing. Parking fees can be an effective instrument to influence commute travel, but for through-travelers and those who can vary the length of time parked, parking fees may have limited or even perverse effects on congestion (Glazer and Niskanen, 1992). A concern when manipulating parking fees for policy purposes is the potential to trigger shifts in the locations of trips themselves, and with them the economic opportunity that trips represent, leading to economic dislocation.

Types of Parking Pricing Strategies

Types of parking pricing strategies include:

Fee Increases and Decreases. Under this strategy, overall rates in an area are changed from a pre-existing level for all users. This occurrence may be a reflection of market forces, may be directed by government policy or regulation, or may be the result of imposed taxes or surcharges.

Short- Versus Long-Term Fee Differentials. With this strategy, the fee structure is typically shaped to favor short-term over long-term use, to eliminate discount rates which attract commuters, and/or to preserve parking capacity for shoppers or other non-commute purposes.

On-Street Parking Fees. This strategy covers putting a price on curbside parking on urban streets, typically through use of meters. Also included are changes in fee levels, fee structure by location or potentially by time of day, or a mixture of pricing actions combined with a broader parking management strategy, such as residential permit parking involving a fee.

Elimination of Employer Parking Subsidy. The great majority of employees are currently provided with free or subsidized parking by employers. Under this strategy, fees are imposed, often in conjunction with offsetting incentives or options to mitigate the disruption for employees, including cash-out and vouchers. The elimination of free parking is often implemented along with other Travel Demand Management (TDM) strategies.

Employee SOV Versus Rideshare Fee Differential. Single occupant vehicle (SOV) versus High Occupancy Vehicle (HOV) fee differentials shape the pricing structure to reward employees who rideshare with lower parking rates than charged those who drive alone. This strategy is often combined with parking supply management and other TDM strategies.

Park-and-Ride Pricing. A rather specific type of parking pricing strategy relates to the pricing policy and fee levels applied at park-and-ride lots, primarily those lots serving transit trips. Park-and-ride pricing may include the imposition of changes in parking fees at park-and-ride lots, as strategies to influence the use of lots, auto occupancy at lots, or the use of transit either as the line-haul or access mode to the lot. Park-and-ride pricing is covered within Chapter 3, "Park-and-Ride/Pool," in the "Underlying Traveler Response Factors" – "User Costs and Willingness to Pay" and "Related Information and Impacts" – "Parking Pricing at Park-and-Ride Facilities" subsections, and is only identified here.

Analytical Considerations

Evidence on travel impacts of parking pricing may be drawn from the following types of sources:

- "Before and after" studies, where parking charges are changed or imposed in an area, site, or group of parking sites;

- "With and without" studies that compare sites (usually work sites) that are similar in all respects but parking charges; and

- Mode choice and travel demand models estimated from travel survey data, where the coefficients or elasticities isolate the effect of parking cost from other decision variables.

The elasticities and traveler responses presented in this chapter have been drawn from each type of source, so interpretation requires some care on the part of the reader. In each case, attention should be paid to the following (Feeney, 1989):

- The definition of what it is that's being measured or estimated – demand for parking at a site or demand for automobile use or probability of choosing the auto mode of travel.

- Potential substitution effects between elements of parking demand – raising prices may stimulate demand for short-term parking at the expense of long term-parking, for example.

- The costs and availability of competing transportation options.

- Possible supply effects – the availability of alternative parking locations.

In practice, relatively little "pure" information exists on the impact of parking pricing, since it is often implemented in concert with parking supply measures and/or additional TDM strategies. The influence of these factors must be kept in mind both when evaluating an individual case and when comparing different situations.

In the section on "Use of the Handbook" within Chapter 1, "Introduction," additional guidance is provided on using generalizations and examples from this *Traveler Response to Transportation System Changes* Handbook. Please note also that throughout the Handbook, because of rounding, figures may not sum exactly to totals provided, and percentages may not add to exactly 100.

Traveler Response Summary

Research appears to corroborate conventional wisdom that parking demand, as measured strictly by number of cars parking (parking facility entries), is inelastic with respect to price. Empirically derived as well as modeled parking demand elasticities for areawide changes in parking price generally range from -0.1 to -0.6, with -0.3 being the most frequently cited value.[1] Most such elasticities have been established on the basis of commuter (work purpose) travel, with very limited useful information on the sensitivity of non-work travel to the price of parking.

Some insight on non-commuter parking is offered by a single study of effects at San Francisco parking facilities of a 25 percent parking tax levy in the early 1970s. An average demand elasticity was found of -0.30 (change in number of autos parking in relation to change in price) across a presumed mix of uses in all facilities. Underlying that average, however, a more complex relationship was revealed, where different classes of users have different choices. Shoppers exhibited ability to adjust their duration of parking in response to higher hourly rates. Commuters, in contrast, could not easily adjust their parking duration and showed less flexibility aside from the fundamental choice of parking at a facility or not. Thus while average demand elasticities of -0.48 were observed in municipal garages primarily serving commuters versus -0.19 in shopper-oriented garages — seemingly contradicting conventional wisdom that shopping and other discretionary travel is more sensitive to price changes than commute travel — price elasticities with respect to gross parking income were found to be in the elastic range, and much closer to each other. The gross parking income elasticities (a surrogate for vehicle-hours-parked elasticities) averaged -1.66 for commuter-oriented garages and -1.30 for shopper-oriented garages in this single case study.

Parking demand price elasticities for individual employment sites and locales, while only marginally supportive of even -0.30 as an average elasticity transferable from areawide to site-specific applications, are nonetheless accompanied by significant shifts in employee mode of travel. Reported employee parking elasticities, some of which may be computationally suspect, lie in the range of -0.1 to -0.3. However, seven case studies in particular, with reported parking

---

[1] An elasticity of -0.3 indicates a 0.3 percent reduction (increase) in parking demand in response to each 1 percent parking fee increase (decrease), calculated in infinitesimally small increments. The negative sign indicates that the effect operates in the opposite direction from the cause. An "elastic" value is -1.0 or beyond, and indicates a demand response that is more than proportionate to the change in the impetus. Elasticities reported in this chapter are thought to be log arc elasticities, unless otherwise noted, and if not are almost certainly closely equivalent computations (see "Concept of Elasticity" in Chapter 1, "Introduction," and Appendix A, "Elasticity Discussion and Formulae").

price elasticities averaging -0.15, also revealed a decline in employees driving cars to work from 72 to 53 percent, a substantial drop in auto use in comparison to other policies with a trip reduction objective. Price elasticity can be a deceptive gauge when taken at face value without applying it to a particular price change situation.

Observed elasticity values in the upper "inelastic" range have occasionally been reported, and even values in the "elastic" range of over -1.0. In some of these instances, the higher elasticity values may reflect changes in total vehicle hours parked or revenues rather than the number of autos parked, as in the case of the San Francisco gross parking income elasticities. In other cases, there may simply have been parking substitutes readily available, such as reasonably priced alternative facilities or free parking off-site, either off- or on-street. Such experiences highlight the potential for parkers to shift parking location, change parking duration, or otherwise avoid parking price increases rather than to shift mode or forego travel. In addition to setting and availability of parking substitutes, other factors such as transit availability and concurrent incentives or programs will also influence traveler response to parking pricing, as will personal income when viewed from the individual traveler perspective.

Nevertheless, because parking demand is normally inelastic with respect to price, imposition of or increases in parking fees are generally met with an increase in total revenue, albeit less than proportionate to the fee change. Such revenue increases do not necessarily accrue to the parking operator, however, if the increase in fees is due to a tax.

Parking rate differentials between short and longer term parking, sometimes combined with supply management strategies or imposition of off- or on-street parking fees, have been successful in reserving parking spaces for short-term users such as midday shoppers or business trips. Off-street parking fee surcharges or increases directed at commuter parking and also residential area on-street parking non-resident fees, in the range of $1.00 to almost $2.00 daily, have been found to decrease peak accumulation or reduce long-term parking by some 20 to 50 percent. Once again, much of the impact observed as a response to such strategies is often attributable to shifts in parking location or behavior rather than changes in mode or travel demand.

Much of the evidence on traveler response to parking pricing is concentrated on the work trip, where the demand for travel and the duration of parking are more or less fixed. Nationwide, only 5 percent of auto commuters pay for parking. Parking pricing for the commute is thus often implemented in the context of TDM programs focused on reducing SOV travel, increasing average vehicle occupancy, or increasing the availability of short-term parking. The mechanism used in such cases is typically some form of elimination of employer parking subsidies. Despite low price elasticities for commuter parking, in 18 work site case studies, the SOV mode share decreased by an average of 21 *percentage points* in response to significant parking pricing strategies. In some of these cases, removal or "cash-out" of employer subsidies was accompanied by subsidies for use of alternative travel modes.

Charging for workplace parking does not automatically translate into large gains for transit usage. Depending on how the pricing is implemented, the setting, and the extent to which ridesharing subsidies are offered, carpool or overall HOV mode share may increase more than transit share. Of 8 case study sites in the Los Angeles Area, while the SOV mode share decreased by 13 percentage points on average, HOV mode share increased by 9 percentage points, while transit mode share increased by 3 percentage points.

On the other hand, logic and some evidence suggest that quality of transit service may significantly affect SOV trip reduction potential. One set of model-derived estimates shows SOV work trip reduction as varying from 10 percent where transit would be poorest (suburbs of small cities with below-average transit service) to 36 percent where transit would be best (core areas of large cities with above-average transit service). Charging for employee parking without reasonable levels of transit service can be expected to produce limited effect on travel and to act primarily as a parking revenue generation strategy.

Though elimination of parking subsidies may have significant impacts at specific work sites, its potential trip reduction impact at a regional level, as an isolated strategy, may be more modest. Theoretical studies have predicted, for example, regional VMT impacts ranging from -1.1 to -2.9 percent for work trip parking pricing. Model-derived analyses also suggest that parking pricing impacts, as measured by SOV trip reduction, may be as much as eight times greater for trip makers in the lowest income quintile as for travelers in the highest quintile.

Evidence from TDM studies suggests that TDM programs based on carefully balanced cost incentive/disincentive actions and offering realistic travel alternatives tend not only to have visibly greater effect on employee vehicle trip rates, but also to sustain those changes over time. In terms of cost-effectiveness, analysis of 49 employer programs indicates that trip reduction without parking pricing requires an expenditure on the part of the employer of over $2.00 per employee commute trip reduced. In contrast, TDM programs with nominal pricing require a lesser expenditure of $0.50 per trip reduced, while sites with parking rates resembling market prices actually result in net revenue of $0.96 for the employer per trip reduced. If the avoided cost of employee parking is included for employers where relevant, the estimated savings with market rate parking are increased more than threefold, and costs become savings for parking priced at nominal rates.

RESPONSE BY TYPE OF STRATEGY

Changes in Overall Parking Rates

The impact of parking pricing in an area will be greatly influenced by the overall supply of parking, including the availability of both on-street and off-street alternatives. The degree to which employers in the area subsidize employee parking will also play a role. There are relatively few documented examples of simple changes in overall parking rates, either at a specific site or set of parking sites or within a broader area.

Areawide Tax or Surcharge

One frequently cited example that is available comes from a 1974 study of a 25 percent areawide parking tax in San Francisco. The tax was imposed in October 1970 on all public and private off-street parking in the city, with the exception of residential spaces. Metered on-street parking was unaffected. Elasticities of demand for parking with respect to price were calculated with an *ex post facto* analysis of parking and revenue data. Results for a sample of 13 municipally operated garages are shown in Table 13-1. The full tax was in effect over a two-year period. Table 13-1 indicates the effect on parking demand in commuter and shopper garages when the tax was in place, first in 1970-71, again in 1971-72, and finally in 1972-73 when the tax was lowered from 25 to 10 percent.

Table 13-1 Price Elasticity of Demand for Parking at San Francisco Municipal Garages

Year	Tax Status	Commuter Garages	Shopper Garages	All Garages
FY 1970-71	25% tax increase in effect	-0.27	-0.08	-0.20
FY 1971-72	25% tax increase in effect	-0.26	-0.25	-0.31
FY 1972-73	Tax decreased to 10%	-0.91	-0.23	-0.38

Notes: Elasticities were calculated on the basis of the number of cars parked, using the log arc formulation and controlling for secular (background) income and parking growth trends.

Source: Kulash (1974).

The elasticities calculated on the basis of the number of autos parked corroborate conventional wisdom that parking demand is inelastic with respect to price. In addition to the values presented in Table 13-1, an overall average "cars-parked" elasticity of about -0.3 was derived. The 13 garages in the sample used in Table 13-1 were also separated into two groups, those used mainly by commuters and those used mainly by shoppers and recreational travelers, as distinguished by parking turnover rates. This permitted analysis of different behaviors of these two types of users. The garages serving predominantly commuters showed somewhat greater sensitivity to parking price than did those serving primarily shoppers, based on number of cars parked, as Table 13-1 illustrates. When the San Francisco parking tax was later reduced, elasticities in the same general range were again observed for the shopper garages, but were more than 3 times higher for commuters, signifying a major rebound in commuter use when parking price dropped.

These "cars-parked" elasticities, however, belie a much more important relationship that was actually occurring in parking demand in response to the tax. When the change in gross parking revenues is examined in relation to the change in price, a much more substantial change is seen, and in fact demonstrates an elastic relationship between gross income and price. Gross income may be taken as a surrogate for vehicle hours parked.

While parking demand (autos parked) in relation to price for commuters yielded an elasticity of about -0.27 in the first year of the tax levy, the elasticity for gross income was -1.50. For shoppers, the elasticity of -0.08 for cars parked was matched with an elasticity for gross income of -1.23. What these findings illustrate is that parking demand is a more complex phenomenon than simply a decision of whether or not to park. In San Francisco, shoppers faced with a higher unit cost for parking chose simply to reduce their duration of parking, whereas commuters – who could not as readily adjust their duration – tended to stop using the given facility entirely (Kulash, 1974). Readers should examine the case study, "A Parking Tax in the City of San Francisco" toward the end of this chapter for a more complete discussion of this traveler response and other aspects of the analysis.

Calculation of elasticities for a set of privately owned San Francisco garages during the same period showed somewhat lower elasticity values, a finding clouded by the reported absorption of a portion of the tax by some sub-optimally located private operators anxious to retain customers. The study also found higher elasticity values for surface lots, both municipal and private. The higher sensitivities were attributed largely to location, because most of the lots were less centrally located than the garages. The elasticity of number of cars parked with respect to price for a sample of 30 municipal surface lots averaged -0.82. In other findings, net garage revenues (less the tax) actually decreased after the imposition of the parking tax due to the shorter average parking durations. The study concluded that while there had been some dampening of traffic growth in San Francisco it was probably not primarily attributable to the parking tax, but that there had been significant impact on parking operator revenue (Kulash, 1974).

Beyond the elasticities and insights available from the San Francisco study, no further empirical information on non-work purpose parking has been encountered. However, for shopping centers, a theoretical study of trip reduction strategies in California offers some noteworthy perspectives. Impact estimates were prepared for real-world regional shopping centers, using an elasticity of -0.34 from the literature, in combination with surveyed parking behavior and stated intentions (what the shoppers said they would do if pricing was imposed). On the basis of change from no or very nominal user parking cost to costs in the range of 38 to 50 cents, parking pricing was predicted to be the most effective of several trip reduction measures studied, but not without unwanted side effects. The projected reduction in vehicle trips to the shopping centers ranged from 27 to 60 percent, but with the major change in behavior being estimated diversion of shoppers to other locations. Without shifts to shopping elsewhere, the projected vehicle trip reduction would have been in the 7.1 to 10.5 percent range. Larger reductions in parking demand, as contrasted to vehicle trip reduction, were foreseen as a result of shoppers parking off site (JHK & Associates et al, 1993).[2]

The range of other areawide parking price elasticity determinations conforms, in general, with the empirically derived overall San Francisco price elasticity of -0.3 for number of cars parked. A mid-1970s study of commuter (work purpose) travel mode choices in metropolitan Toronto derived an elasticity of -0.31. Estimates prepared with work trip destination and mode choice modeling, utilizing a 1995 household and travel-activity survey for Portland, Oregon, produced elasticity values that varied considerably by the assumed base price. At a base price of $80 per month, the price elasticity of demand for commuter parking in urban Portland was estimated to be -0.58 for SOVs and -0.43 for carpools. Corresponding suburban Portland values were -0.46 for SOVs and -0.44 for carpools (Dueker, Strathman and Bianco, 1998). A lower charge might well be more relevant in many urban sectors, and certainly in suburban areas. The same analysis at a base price of $20 per month obtained SOV commuter parking elasticities of -0.12 for urban Portland and -0.09 for suburban Portland and -0.11 for urban and suburban carpool use. Modeled values for other base prices were arrayed in between (Portland State University, 1995).

---

[2] Another perspective is now provided by stated preference experiments conducted of casual parkers and transit riders in downtown Sydney, Australia, and modeling based thereon. Casual parkers were defined as those without guaranteed parking, subsidized or not. Elasticities of -0.541, -1.015, and -0.476 were obtained for centrally located casual parking (heavily business related), parking elsewhere in the CBD (more shopping/social-recreational), and in the CBD fringe. Logit model scenario testing of parking fee increases produced estimates of significant shifts to public transit, and shifts from centrally located to other CBD and outside-of-CBD parking, but negligible loss in travel to the CBD (Hensher and King, 2001). Major differences between this CBD environment and regional shopping centers are much better transit service and proportionally more business travel.

Reported worksite parking price elasticities, covered in full under "Elimination of Employer Parking Subsidy," are -0.32 or less. Despite the relatively low reported elasticities of parking demand in response to price changes, parking pricing does appear to be capable of producing significant impacts at specific employment sites and locales. The "Elimination of Employer Parking Subsidy" subsection provides information about the effects on employee mode shares and rates of auto use for commuting.

Supply, Demand, Price, and Mode Share

Data which illustrate the relationship between parking supply, demand, and price at an areawide level are scarce, as previously mentioned. The data displayed in Table 13-2 below offer a profile of these interrelationships across a number of U.S. cities, specifically in relation to commute travel to regional central business districts (CBDs). In most instances, where parking is constrained (low ratio of spaces per employee), market prices for parking are higher and SOV use is lower. Exceptions exist and raise the question of the relative importance of parking availability (including private and/or on-street) versus price, prevalence of employee parking subsidies, quality of transit service, cost of living, and other factors.

Table 13-2 Parking in CBD Areas of U.S. Cities: Availability, Price, and Utilization

City	Off-Street Spaces per Employee	Average Monthly Parking Price	Percent Commute Trips by SOV
Philadelphia	0.17	$165	14%
Baltimore	0.22	95	64
Pittsburgh	0.30	n/a	45*
Portland	0.39	105	52
Honolulu	0.40	104	59
Minneapolis	0.44	80	68
Indianapolis	0.47	n/a	87*
Denver	0.52	75	54
Atlanta	0.53	50	49
Madison	0.58	50	61
San Diego	0.58	130	88
Los Angeles	0.68	n/a	40
Phoenix	0.73	n/a	70
Charlotte	0.76	n/a	70

Note: Asterisked figures (*) include carpool use.

Source: Urban Transportation Monitor (April 2, 1993).

A 1986 survey of market parking prices, employer parking subsidies, and commuter mode shares in five different subareas of downtown Los Angeles also illustrates relationships between parking prices and mode share. As shown in Table 13-3, higher parking prices are, in general, associated with lower SOV shares and somewhat higher transit shares in cases where employees pay for parking. Where employers subsidize parking, these associations cannot be readily discerned and SOV shares are higher.

Table 13-3 Data Summary - Sensitivity of Mode Share to Parking Subsidy Policy, by Los Angeles Subarea

Location and Avg. Parking Price:		Mode Share Percentage					
		Financial Core ($121)	Bunker Hill ($100)	Civic Center ($84)	Broadway —Spring ($73)	South Park ($59)	Entire Study Area ($85)
All Employers	SOV	62%	70%	60%	39%	67%	61%
	HOV	12	11	22	16	18	15
	Transit	25	16	17	40	15	22
	(# cases)	(870)	(1,314)	(2,225)	(448)	(155)	(5,012)
Free Parking (Subsidized)	SOV	67%	85%	65%	73%	68%	71%
	HOV	10	5	18	27	21	13
	Transit	22	5	17	0	11	13
	(# cases)	(216)	(74)	(418)	(4)	(27)	(739)
No Subsidies	SOV	56%	42%	51%	39%	77%	54%
	HOV	7	14	28	0	11	8
	Transit	35	45	20	61	11	36
	(# cases)	(72)	(268)	(126)	(22)	(18)	(506)

Notes: The number of cases reported is for all modes in that subarea, unweighted. The mode share percentages use weighted survey responses. Parking costs are derived from a 1986 market survey. Parking subsidy characteristics were estimated from survey data.

Source: Shoup (1990).

Results are available for a case in Eugene, Oregon, where rates were raised at two municipal garages and several surface parking lots over a one-year period. Garage rates increased from $16 to $30 per month, while surface lot rates increased from $6-16 to $16-34 per month. At the same time, fines for commuters parking in short-term metered spaces were increased. Monthly parking permit sales fell from 560 to 360. Half of the former parkers switched to carpools or rode a free shuttle, and half changed parking locations (Peat, Marwick, Mitchell, 1985). The log arc elasticity of monthly permit sales with respect to monthly rates was on the order of -0.6.

Short- Versus Long-Term Differentials

Short- versus long-term parking pricing differentials are typically implemented at activity centers where there is mid-day versus all-day competition for spaces and/or where parking is limited. This strategy might be implemented, for example, to provide improved parking space availability for attracting more shoppers and non-workers to a downtown during the day.

Peak-Period Surcharge

A 1980-81 peak-period pricing demonstration in Madison, Wisconsin, aimed to discourage commuting by private vehicle with the ultimate objective of freeing more spaces for mid-day shopping and personal business trips. The pricing consisted of a peak-period charge of $1.00

levied on all parkers entering between 7:00 and 9:30 a.m., and staying for more than three hours, at three of the five public parking facilities that were part of the demonstration. Except for the peak-period surcharge, the parking price of 20¢ per hour remained the same. The surcharged facilities represented 22 percent of Madison's public, off-street parking inventory, including metered and attended spaces in lots and garages. Free shuttle buses to fringe parking lots were instituted prior to the peak-period charge.

The peak-period surcharge resulted in a 40 percent decrease in the number of spaces occupied at the surcharged facilities during the peak period. To gauge the effects of the surcharge on travel behavior, a panel of parkers who had used the facilities before the surcharge began was contacted and asked about their travel behavior during a one week period, as compared to before imposition of the surcharge. Table 13-4 lists the most commonly reported travel behavior changes that were made by those individuals one or more times during the week, along with the percentage of respondents attributing the change to the surcharge. The two most common responses were changing to a different parking location and changing to a metered space at the same location. Relatively few of the individuals who had parked in one of the surcharge facilities switched to one of the fringe parking facilities opened as part of the demonstration (Charles River Associates, 1984).

Table 13-4   Change in Travel Behavior Resulting from Peak-Period Surcharge in Madison, Wisconsin

Reported Change in Behavior	Number in Sample Reporting (percent)	Percent Attributing Change to Surcharge
Changed Parking Facility	96 (35%)	64%
Parked at Meter in Same Facility	5 (2)	86
Used Another Mode	50 (18)	54
Left Within Three Hours	44 (15)	18
Rode as Passenger	39 (14)	41
Changed Time Entering Facility	37 (13)	65
Drove With Others	37 (13)	24
Stopped Coming Downtown	37 (13)	3

Notes: The sample size was 278 and multiple responses were possible.

Source: Charles River Associates (1984).

Additional information on the Madison peak-period surcharge is presented in the case study, "Madison Peak-Period Parking Pricing Demonstration."

Increase in Rate Differential

A study of rate increases at city-owned parking facilities in Chicago examined the effect of parking rate changes on the number, duration, and accumulation of vehicles in eight municipal garages. The new short-term rates were less than those at nearby privately owned garages, and the new long-term rates were similar, as shown in Table 13-5.

Table 13-5 Differential Rate Increases at Chicago Parking Garages

| Time Period | Median Rates at Municipal Garages | | | Median Rates at Comparable Private Facilities |
	Before Increase	After Increase	Percent Change	
1 hour	$ 0.90	$ 1.15	28%	$1.75
8 hour	2.15	4.03	87%	4.05
Monthly	30.50	58.00	90%	n/a

Source: Kunze, Heramb and Martin (1980) and calculations by Handbook authors.

The study found that long-term parking decreased by about 50 percent overall, and by 72 percent for vehicles arriving before 9:30 AM on weekdays. Table 13-6 illustrates the shift in parking patterns. As shown, the percentage of all cars parked accounted for by short-term (0-3 hour) parkers increased from 34 to 47 percent. On the other hand, the change in short-term parking use was small in absolute numbers. Long-term (3-24 hours) parking use decreased significantly in both percentage and absolute terms. The use of monthly parking also decreased, although the percentage accounted for by monthly parkers remained relatively constant.

Table 13-6 Change in Parking Patterns at Chicago Parking Facilities

| Time Period | Change from Use in Base Year (percent) | | Percentage of All Cars Parked | | |
	1978	1979	Base	1978	1979
0-3 hours	+2%	+1%	34%	49%	47%
3-24 hours	-50	-50	47	32	32
Monthly	-27	-24	18	18	19
All	-27%	-24%			

Source: Kunze, Heramb and Martin (1980).

The fee-induced changes in parking patterns were still evident 17 months after the increase. Although the absolute number of parkers had decreased, revenue generated by the eight city garages increased. The effects on the amount and duration of parking, rate structures, and revenues at privately owned facilities were found to be minimal. In the opinion of the study's authors, former long-term parkers shifted from parking at city facilities to using transit (Kunze, Heramb and Martin, 1980). Using the data from this study, a log arc price elasticity of -1.2 for long-term parking has been calculated (Feeney, 1989). This atypically elastic response to a parking price change is probably explained by the circumstance that the price increase brought municipal garage rates up to par with private garages, making them direct substitutes.

On-Street Parking Pricing

Metering or charging for on-street parking is often implemented to combat low turnover (number of cars served by a space) and consequent lack of on-street parking availability. New technology, such as variable-priced meters allowing changes in rates by time of day, is providing added flexibility (Valk, 1999). No studies of behavioral changes in response to such technology are yet known to exist, however, and impact studies are extremely scarce even for conventional on-street parking pricing (See footnote 3.)

According to a study of Boston area parking management, need to reevaluate on-street parking prices for probable upward adjustment is indicated by double parking, obstruction of loading zones, other illegal parking, or traffic generated by vehicles seeking on-street parking. Prices lower for on- street than off-street parking, as well as off-street parking rates which disadvantage short- and intermediate-term parkers, may also indicate a need to revamp the pricing structure. The study authors stress that off-street parking rates should be more attractive to long-term parkers than on-street rates and that enforcement of on-street parking regulations is crucial to success (Laube and Dansker, 1983).

A preferential parking pricing program in Eugene, Oregon, offers some evidence of the effects on travel behavior from application of combined parking supply management and pricing of on-street parking as do additional programs discussed in Chapter 18, "Parking Management and Supply." To combat low turnover and high usage of street parking spaces by non-residents in predominately residential areas, Eugene established three parking zones. Residents holding permits could enjoy unlimited parking in the respective areas, while non-resident commuters, students, and others were restricted to two-hour limits. In two of the three zones, non-residents were permitted to buy monthly or daily permits for unlimited parking, at a cost of $10 to $17.50 per month, or $1.50 per day. Results of this program were as shown in Table 13-7. Turnover went down in one zone and up in two, remaining about the same on average. The number of cars parked at any given time and parking duration (length of stay) were both reduced in all three zones.

Table 13-7   Summary of Eugene, Oregon, Residential Parking Management and Pricing Program Effects (Percent Change)

Area	Program	Cars Parked	Duration	Turnover
Zone B	Residential Permit 2-Hr. Limit for Non-Resident	-50%	-30%	-29%
Zone C	Residential Permit 2-Hr. Limit for Non-Resident Non-Resident Permit Option	-33	-39	+8
Zone D	Residential Permit 2-Hr. Limit for Non-Resident Non-Resident Permit Option	-22	-36	+21

Notes: Cars Parked is the number parked at any one given time (parking accumulation). Duration is average length of stay (time parked). Turnover is average number of cars served by a space in a day.

Source: Dornan and Keith (1988).

(See footnote 3, next page, for one new study.)

While this program was reasonably successful in achieving its objectives of freeing up on-street parking for residents and short-term users, most of the change was accomplished through modifications in parking behavior. Ninety-five percent of non-residents continued to drive alone to the area (rather than shift mode), but either parked in private facilities or managed their parking time to stay within the two hour limit. Pricing through permits seems to have had a very minor role, as only 41 monthly permits and 157 daily permits were sold in an average month, accounting for only about 50 users a day. This compares to a perceived shortage of about 1,000 on-street parking spaces prior to the program (Dornan and Keith, 1988).[3]

Elimination of Employer Parking Subsidy

The role of employer-provided parking as a contributor to high rates of SOV use by employees has received considerable attention. In particular, the long-established ability of employers to subsidize employee parking as a deductible business expense under U.S. federal tax law has been frequently challenged. Transit and environmental advocates have held this to be an unfair advantage for auto use; an advantage that was most obvious before some degree of alternative mode tax-free employer subsidy was also allowed. One study has estimated that, considering employer and all other subsidies, commuters on average avoid direct payment of 85 percent of the true cost of parking, although some employees may also pay in hidden, indirect ways (Portland State University, 1995). This raises the question of what would happen to mode shares if subsidies to employee parking were reduced or eliminated.

Case Studies and Observations

The 1990 Nationwide Personal Transportation Study (NPTS) survey found that over 95 percent of all automobile commuters park free (Shoup 1990, 1994a, 1994b, 1997). Since free employee parking is primarily the result of employer subsidies, elimination of these subsidies is often targeted as part of both mandatory and voluntary trip reduction programs. In fact, much of the reported research has stemmed from employer TDM initiatives, influenced by either traffic or growth management ordinances, and air quality programs. Parking costs and SOV usage rates are inversely related for the most part (Rutherford et al, 1995). Research has shown parking pricing to be one of the more effective TDM strategies:

- Monthly on-site parking cost was found to be the factor most highly correlated with employee automobile use at six San Francisco, California, health care sites (Dowling, Feltham and Wycko, 1991). Correlation coefficients of -0.85 to -0.91 were obtained in this analysis (where -1.00 signifies a perfect inverse relationship between price level and auto use level).

- A review of 22 individual TDM programs showed a very strong relationship between the existence of priced and/or restricted parking and lower rates of vehicle trip generation. The programs were compared to situations similar except for lack of parking pricing and restraints, or to conditions before the parking charge was introduced (see Table 13-8).

---

[3] A more conventional but instructive on-street parking pricing application in Pasadena, California, newly documented as of this chapter's final publication, is evolutionary in practical application but revolutionary in its use of parking revenues. Pasadena's historic CBD suffered a 50-year decline starting in 1930. Its initial revival as "Old Pasadena" was hampered by low availability of curb parking spaces. Businesses and owners were convinced to approve high-rate parking meters when the commitment was made to plow net revenues back into local-area pedestrian-friendly public amenities and services. Meters were installed in 1993, charging $1.00/hour, evenings and Sundays included. A 2001 study found an average curb-space occupancy of 83 percent, ideal to ensure shopper parking availability. Sales tax revenue, which had already started climbing, roughly tripled between 1993 and 1999. In contrast, similar Westwood Village in West Los Angeles halved its meter rate to $0.50/hour in 1994, creating a perceived parking shortage (96 percent peak curb space occupancy) even as off-street spaces were only 68 percent full (Kolozsvari and Shoup, 2003).

Table 13-8   Relation of Trip Reduction Rates to Parking Charges in 22 TDM Programs

Program Net Trip Reduction	Parking Charges		Restricted Parking Supply	
	No	Yes	No	Yes
Greater than 30%	1	5	1	5
15 to 30%	2	7	0	9
Less than 15%	5	2	4	3

Note: Table gives number of programs in each cross-classification.

Source: Comsis and ITE (1993).

TCRP Project B-4, "Cost Effectiveness of Travel Demand Management (TDM) Strategies," investigated TDM programs at 49 employment sites with the objective of determining which types of strategieswere most cost-effective. When the vehicle trip generation rates at the selected sites were compared with ambient vehicle trip rates from the 1990 Census Transportation Planning Package (CTPP), those sites whose TDM programs included parking pricing showed significantly lower relative rates of employee vehicle trip generation than those where parking was not priced. As indicated in Table 13-9, those 10 sites that charged "market rates" for parking had vehicle trip rates that averaged 32.2 percent below ambient levels, and those 10 sites that had nominal rates (at least some user charge, but below market rates) averaged 17.9 percent below ambient. In contrast, the remaining 29 TDM program sites, which imposed no price for parking, averaged only 8.4 percent below ambient trip rates. In fact, of these 29 cases with free parking, eight TDM programs actually had vehicle trip rates greater than or equal to ambient rates (Comsis, 1994).

Table 13-9   Use of Parking Pricing Compared with Trip Generation Rates for 49 TDM Programs

Parking Fee	Number of TDM Sites with Trip Rate Below Ambient Rate by Indicated Percent					Average Pct. Below Ambient
	Higher/Same as Ambient	1 to 6%	7 to 15%	16 to 29%	30% or more	
Market Rates	0	0	1	3	5	32.2%
Nominal Rates	2	1	2	1	4	17.9%
Free	8	9	7	3	2	8.4%

Source: Comsis (1994).

Apart from studies of TDM programs, a number of case studies of work trip parking pricing have been conducted, of both the "before and after" as well as the "with and without" variety. Table 13-10 summarizes a series of observations of area wide parking pricing effects at seven locations, over the period 1969 through the early 1990s. The table shows the difference in SOV mode share and vehicle trip generation rates for sites where the employer pays for parking as compared to sites where the user pays (Shoup, 1994a).

Table 13-10 Case Studies of Parking Pricing Effects at Seven Employment Locations

Location, Date (Type of Case Study)	Solo Driver Mode Share			Cars per 100 Employees			Price Elasticity of Parking Demand
	Employer Pays for Parking	Driver Pays for Parking	Differ-ence	Employer Pays for Parking	Driver Pays for Parking	Differ-ence	
1. Civic Center, Los Angeles, 1969 (with/without)	72%	40%	-32%	78	50	-28	-0.22
2. Downtown Ottawa, Canada, 1978 (before/after)	35%	28%	-7%	39	62	-7	-0.10
3. Century City, Los Angeles, 1980 (with/without)	92%	75%	-17%	94	80	-14	-0.08
4. Mid-Wilshire, Los Angeles, 1984 (before/after)	42%	8%	-34%	48	30	-18	-0.23
5. Warner Center, Los Angeles, 1989 (before/after)	90%	46%	-44%	92	64	-28	-0.18
6. Washington, DC, 1991 (with/without)	72%	50%	-22%	76	58	-18	-0.13
7. Downtown Los Angeles, 1991 (with/without)	69%	48%	-21%	75	56	-19	-0.15
Average values	67%	42%	-25%	72	53	-19	-0.15

Notes: "With/without" refers to a case study comparing the commuting behavior of employees with and without employer-paid parking. "Before/after" refers to a case study comparing the commuting behavior of employees before and after elimination of employer payment for parking. The estimated price elasticity of demand is the midpoint arc elasticity.

Source: Shoup (1994a).

The price elasticities shown in Table 13-10 are low compared to some of the other studies reported, averaging -0.15 and ranging from a low of -0.08 in Century City to a high of -0.22 in the Los Angeles Mid-Wilshire area. There is concern that at some of these seven locations the elasticities may have been diluted by inclusion of unaffected parties, such as carpool commuters or individual employee groups, without corresponding adjustment of the elasticity computations. In any case, the data show a very considerable difference in auto use between sites with and without user payment for parking.

Earlier before-and-after case studies conducted in Los Angeles and Canada show similar impacts on SOV mode share when employees are charged for parking. Table 13-11 illustrates this and also carpool and transit before and after mode shares. From the data presented in the Canadian case study, a log arc parking price elasticity of demand for driving (including HOV vehicles) can be measured at -0.1 (Feeney, 1989).

Table 13-11 Additional Examples of Charging for Workplace Parking

Mode Share	Canadian Study		Los Angeles Study	
	Before	After	Before	After
Drive alone	35%	28%	55%	30%
Carpool	11	10	13	45
Transit	42	49	29	22
Other	12	13	3	3
Total	100%	100%	100%	100%

Source: Data is from Feeney (1989).

The U.S. government, in November 1979, started requiring federal employees to pay one-half the prevailing rates of commercial garages. A before-and-after analysis of 15 work sites in the Washington, DC, area was carried out using a sample of non-governmental sites as a control. The reduction in the number of autos used for commuting ranged from 1 to 10 percent in central city areas, and between 2 and 4 percent in suburban locations (Miller and Everett, 1982). Price elasticities of demand for work site parking calculated for these sites varied substantially but were relatively low: -0.32 or less (Feeney, 1989).

Strategies for withdrawing the employer parking subsidy can take several different forms. The subsidy may simply be eliminated, requiring employees who drive to work to pay the market rate for parking out-of-pocket. Or, employers may give employees a "transportation allowance" that employees can apply towards the mode of their choice in the form of parking costs, transit passes, or whatever. Transportation allowances may or may not fully cover the cost of parking at a work site. A third option gaining increased attention is employer parking "cash-out," where employees are given the cost of a parking space in cash only if they choose to forego driving. This option is discussed in more detail below. It should be first noted, however, that the option definitions given here are not always closely adhered to. Sometimes employer parking subsidy elimination in any form is included under the "cash-out" rubric.

Parking Cash-Out

In 1992, California enacted "parking cash-out" legislation that required many employers to offer employees the option to choose cash in lieu of any parking subsidy offered. This legislation applies only to large employers that are located in air quality non-attainment areas, who subsidize parking, and can reduce the number of parking spaces leased without penalty. The before-and-after impacts for eight selected employers who complied with the law are summarized in Table 13-12 in terms of mode shifts and vehicle trip and VMT reduction. Overall, the drive alone mode share fell by about 12 *percentage points* after implementation of parking cash-out, while the average commuting subsidy per employee rose by only $2.00 per month (Shoup, 1997).

Table 13-12   Average Parking Cash-Out Travel Impacts for Eight Southern California Case Studies

| | Average Value | | |
Measure	Before	After	Change
Drive Alone Mode Share	76.8%	65.3%	-11.5%-Pts.
Carpool Mode Share	12.9%	20.0%	+7.1%-Pts.
Transit Mode Share	5.8%	8.3%	+2.5%-Pts.
Walk Mode Share	3.1%	4.6%	+1.5%-Pts.
Bicycle Mode Share	1.1%	1.4%	+0.2%-Pts.
Annual Vehicle Trips per Employee	379	335	-11%
Annual VMT per Employee	5348	4697	-12%

Note: Analysis based on employee travel survey data – average of 8 case studies. Average one-way trip distance is 15 miles based on 1991 survey of commuters in the South Coast Air Basin.

Source: Rederivation of findings tabulated in Shoup (1997).

Factors which affect the impact of individual parking cash-out programs include the proportion of employees that are candidates for cash-out, availability of transit, and the presence of uncontrolled parking supplies (K.T. Analytics, 1994). Typically, local regulations also require employers to ensure that employees who cash out do not park elsewhere in the vicinity of the work site. Table 13-13 provides examples of work site pricing schemes that have been used to implement parking cash-out programs (loosely defined), along with mode share impacts. The first eight examples in Table 13-13 are from the case studies summarized in Table 13-12.

Table 13-13 Parking Pricing Details and Mode Choice Impacts for Eleven Subsidy Elimination and Cash-Out Programs

Case Study Location (CA unless noted)	Before					After				
	Monthly Parking Subsidy[a]	Alternative Mode Subsidy[b]	SOV Mode Share	HOV Mode Share	Transit Mode Share[c]	Parking Subsidy /Price[d]	Alternative Mode Subsidy[b]	SOV Mode Share	HOV Mode Share	Transit Mode Share[c]
1. Century City	$110	$55%	$71%	21%	4.5%	$0/110	$55	58%	33%	4.5%
2. West Hollywood	$65	$45	72%	6%	5%	$65/0	$65	70%	4%	2%
3. Century City	$100	$0	79%	13%	8%	$100/0	$100	67%[e]	19%	9%
4. Century City	$120	less than $120[f]	88%	10%	0%	$120/0	$150	76%	18%	5%
5. Downtown Los Angeles	$90-145*	$0	75%	10%	15%	$100/varied	$150	53%	23%	24%
6. Santa Monica	$55	$15 per transit user	85%	7%	1%	$55/0	$55 plus $15 to transit users	78%	8%	2%
7. Santa Monica	$62* per SOV; $77 per carpool	$175 per vanpool; $75 – transit users; $25 – cyclists/peds.	83%	13%	1%	$62/15	$77 or $165 per vanpool	75%	20%	3%
8. Downtown Los Angeles	$30	none	61%	23%	12%	$11/25	$50	45%	35%	15%
9. Los Angeles	$30	Various transit & vanpool subsidies	90%	n/a	n/a	$0/30	Various transit & vanpool subsidies	65%	n/a	n/a
10. Los Angeles County	$70-$120	none	53%	n/a	n/a	$0/70-120	$70*	47%	n/a	n/a
11. Bellevue, WA	$40	none	89%	n/a	n/a	$0/40 for SOV; $40/0 for carpools	$40*	64%	n/a	n/a

Notes:

a Subsidy is the difference between the cost of the space to the employer and what the employee pays for parking. Unless indicated with an asterisk (*), the parking was "free" to the employee (i.e., required no cash outlay from the employee).

b Alternative mode subsidies were paid only to commuters not using a parking space. An asterisk indicates that the amount was a "transportation allowance" paid to all commuters (i.e., applicable toward parking expenses).

c Changes in use of nonmotorized travel, for which mode shares are not shown, occurred in some instances (see also Table 13-12 for first 8 case studies).

d The parking subsidy is paid by employers. The parking price is paid by employees.

e Represents the change over three years.

f Non solo drivers earned "rideshare points" redeemable for prizes.

Sources: First eight case studies – Shoup (1997); last three case studies – K.T. Analytics (1994).

Some Modeled Impacts

Transportation survey data from commuters to downtown Los Angeles were used to estimate commuter response to an increase in cost to employees of the price of parking. The price increase was assumed equal to the after-tax cash value of the tax-exempt parking subsidy each commuter was being offered. As shown in Table 13-14, simple elimination of the parking subsidy (driver pays full price for parking) was predicted to have the greatest impact on SOV use (reduced to 48 percent from 69 percent), as shown in the "Driver Pays for Parking" column. However, the less stringent approach of retaining employer-subsidized parking but also offering a cash-out option to give employees more of a free-market choice (employer pays for parking with cash-out option) was also examined. In this case, as shown in the "With Cash-Out Option" column, SOV use was still estimated to decline by an appreciable amount (to 55 from 69 percent) (Shoup, 1994b).

Table 13-14   Predicted Effect of Parking Subsidy Elimination and Cash-Out Among Los Angeles CBD Commuters

Travel Behavior or Travel Expenditure	Driver Pays for Parking	Employer Pays for Parking	
		With Cash-Out Option	*Without* Cash-Out
Solo Driver Share	48%	55%	69%
Vehicle Trips to Work (Parking Spaces Occupied) (per employee)	0.56	0.62	0.75
Vehicle Miles Traveled (per employee per day)	18.1	20.2	24.1
Gasoline Consumed (gallons/employee per year)	231	258	308
Parking and Auto Use Expenditure (per employee per year)	$1,137	$1,271	$1,517

Notes: The analysis assumed the number of days worked per year (217), auto fuel efficiency (17 mpg), the cost of auto use ($0.29 per mile), and a monthly parking cost ($83.82).

Source: Shoup (1994b). Drawn from analysis of Los Angeles CBD employee survey data and model developed by Willson in "Estimating the Effect of Employer Paid Parking in Downtown Los Angeles," *Regional Science and Urban Economics*, Vol. 22 (1991).

While elimination of parking subsidies appears to have significant impacts at specific work sites, the potential impact at a regional level may be more modest.[4] A 1996 study used sample enumeration techniques, incorporated in a "Short-Range Transportation Evaluation Program" (STEP) model, to assess the impact of various transportation pricing strategies in California, including parking pricing. The analysis assumed that only drive alone commuters would be charged for a space, and the price effect was reflected through adjustments to the average zonal parking price (Deakin et al, 1996). Results for a base year analysis, along with results of a similar analysis carried out for Seattle, Washington, are presented in Table 13-15.

---

[4] Regional dissipation of effects is examined in detail in Chapter 19, "Employer and Institutional TDM Strategies," under "Related Information and Impacts" – "TDM Impact Concentration/Dispersion."

Table 13-15 Modeling of Employee Parking Pricing Regional Impacts

Region	Minimum Price ($)	Weekday VMT (percent)	Weekday Trips (percent)	Weekday Vehicle Hours of Travel (percent)	Weekday Vehicle Hours of Delay (percent)	Daily Gallons of Fuel/Tons of CO_2 (percent)	Daily Tons of Reactive Organic Hydro-carbons (percent)	Daily Tons of CO (percent)	Daily Tons of NOx (percent)
Bay Area (CA)	$1.00	-0.8%	-1.0%	-1.3%	-2.3%	-1.1%	-0.9%	-0.9%	-0.8%
	3.00	-2.3	-2.6	-3.7	-7.0	-2.6	-2.5	-2.6	-2.4
Sacramento (CA)	1.00	-1.1	-1.2	-1.6	-2.5	-1.2	-1.2	-1.2	-1.0
	3.00	-2.9	-3.1	-4.1	-6.0	-3.0	-3.1	-3.1	-2.8
San Diego (CA)	1.00	-1.0	-1.1	-1.5	-2.5	-1.1	-1.0	-1.0	-0.9
	3.00	-2.6	-2.9	-3.8	-6.0	-2.7	-2.8	-2.8	-2.5
South Coast (CA)	1.00	-1.0	-1.1	-1.5	-2.5	-1.2	-1.1	-1.1	-1.0
	3.00	-2.7	-3.0	-4.2	-7.5	-2.9	-2.9	-2.9	-2.7
Seattle (WA)	3.00	-1.9	-2.4	n/a	n/a	-2.2	n/a	n/a	-1.9

Notes: Impacts are calculated from a 1991 baseline scenario for the California case studies and from a 1994 baseline for the Seattle example.

Sources: California – Deakin et al (1996); Seattle – Portland State University (1995).

The predicted base year parking charge impacts proved to be modest; for example, estimated overall VMT reductions for the California regions ranged from -2.3 to -2.9 percent. Yet the reductions were not vastly different than for the other pricing strategies studied, excepting a $2.00 per gallon fuel tax. Table 13-16 shows how employee parking charge impacts compared to those of selected alternative transportation pricing strategies.

Table 13-16 Comparison of Regional Transportation Pricing Strategies - Impact on Regional VMT (Percent Decrease)

Region	Strategy and Percent VMT Decrease				
	Employee Parking Charge ($3.00)	Congestion Pricing (Avg. Price per Mile)	Fuel Tax Increases ($2.00 per gallon)	VMT Fee ($0.02 per mile)	Emissions Fees (Avg. of $0.01/mile over fleet)
Bay Area, CA	-2.3%	-1.8% ($0.09)	-12.6%	-4.2%	-2.0%
Sacramento, CA	-2.9	-0.6 ($0.04)	-13.9	-4.7	-2.7
San Diego, CA	-2.6	-1.0 ($0.06)	-13.2	-4.4	-2.4
South Coast, CA	-2.7	-2.3 ($0.10)	-13.3	-4.4	-2.2
Seattle, WA	-1.9	-1.3	-7.2	-9.3[a]	n/a

Notes: Fuel tax increase numbers for the California regions assume an increase in fuel efficiency from 22 to 28 mpg.

[a] A $0.06 per mile fee was applied in the case of Seattle.

Sources: California – Deakin et al (1996), Seattle – Portland State University (1995).

It should be noted that when this same general type of analysis was carried out for purposes of TCRP Project H-3, the reported results for California differed somewhat and more closely matched those for Seattle. An employee parking charge of $3.00 was estimated to reduce VMT in the San Francisco, Sacramento, San Diego and Los Angeles metropolitan areas by -1.1, -1.8, -1.7 and -1.6 percent, respectively. The impact estimates for other strategies were likewise smaller. VMT Fee impact estimates were not reported (Dueker, Strathman and Bianco, 1998). The conclusions that may be drawn remain roughly the same, despite the differences in the specific estimates: predicted employee parking pricing impacts on vehicular travel were quite modest at a regional level, but slightly more effective than other pricing strategies studied, except for the $2.00 fuel tax.

Tax Code Implications

The impact of eliminating employee parking subsidies or implementing parking cash-out programs is affected by the treatment of employee transportation and parking benefits under the U.S. federal tax code. All experience and findings reported here for elimination of employer parking subsidies were accrued under codes that favored SOV use over other modes by allowing greater tax-free subsidies for parking. Initially, provision of parking was treated as a non-taxable cost of doing business, whereas there was no provision at all for tax-free subsidy to alternative modes, a barrier to parking cash-out programs such as California's. Later, subsidized transportation became a qualified fringe benefit, excluded up to specified inflation-indexed limits from employees' taxable income.

The latest U.S. federal transportation funding bill, TEA 21, enacted in 1998, raises the maximum monthly tax-free cap for transit and vanpool transportation from $65 per month (plus inflation adjustment) to $100 per month in 2002. The employee avoids income tax on the commute transportation payment, whether it is in lieu of wages or an outright fringe benefit. Parking cash-out is thus facilitated because employers may let employees who elect to cash out the value of their parking benefit to choose, without penalty, a tax-free transit or vanpool payment or taxable cash. Transit and vanpool benefits within the specified caps may be set aside on a pre-tax basis such that the employer avoids certain federal, state and local taxes on the benefits (Association for Commuter Transportation, 1999).

Employee SOV Versus Rideshare Fee Differentials

The pure effect of reducing or eliminating the parking fees charged to carpools and vanpools is difficult to determine because this strategy is often instituted (or dropped) along with other employee parking price changes and TDM strategies. For example, at a company in Santa Monica, California, SOV shares fell even as the vanpool subsidy was reduced and free parking for carpools was eliminated, presumably because this was done together with implementation of a parking cash-out policy.

Table 13-17 exhibits 10 employers observed in TCRP Project B-4 as sites where differential (lower) rates were charged to rideshare vehicles (HOVs). In some cases, there was simply a different parking fee for SOVs as compared to HOVs, though in most cases the HOV rate was graduated to produce higher discounts and greater incentive to those vehicles with more occupants. Also, in some instances, the differential rate for HOVs was accomplished directly through the parking price itself (such as at Hartford Steam Boiler and US WEST), while at other sites it was reflected in specific alternate mode subsidies or transportation allowances (such as at City/County of Denver). In still other cases, parking rate differentials were accompanied by differences in location or availability of parking; for example, US WEST provides guaranteed reserved parking for HOVs in the company garage, while SOVs may only park on a daily, first come-first served basis (Comsis, 1994).

Site vehicle trip rates for the 10 employers averaged 32 percent lower than ambient trip rates. The lower trip rates are attributable to the overall packages of TDM strategies employed, however, not solely to the HOV parking fee differentials and preferences.

One effect often seen when parking costs for rideshare vehicles are subsidized is an increase in carpool and vanpool use at the expense of transit mode share. In one case study in Los Angeles, parking charges of $57.50 per month were imposed on solo drivers but parking remained free to carpoolers. The carpool share rose from 17 to 58 percent while the transit share declined from 38 to 28 percent. This change was explained as the result of solo drivers inviting former transit users to share their cars in order to continue to receive free parking (Shoup, 1994b).

In another case, two Los Angeles employers in identical adjacent buildings were found to have almost the same drive alone mode shares (49-48 percent), but the transit share at one site was 31 percent as compared to 18 percent at the other. The company with the higher transit share charged all drivers $60 per month, while the company with the lower share charged solo drivers $50 a month, 2-person carpools $25 a month, and 3+ carpools and vanpools nothing, with a vanpool rider travel allowance thrown in (Mehranian et al, 1987). This naturally occurring quasi-experiment is elaborated on in the case study, "Contrasting Approaches to Parking Pricing in Downtown Los Angeles."

Table 13-17 Ten Employer Sites with Differential Parking Prices or Subsidies for SOV and HOV

Employer/Location	Parking Pricing	Subsidies	Vehicle Trip Rate *per capita*	Ambient Trip Rate *per capita*	Site vs. Ambient Trip Rate
Hartford Steam Boiler Hartford, CT, CBD	$110/month SOV $75/month carpool-2 $40/month carpool-3 $10/month carpool-4+	50% transit subsidy	0.49	0.77	-36.4%
GEICO Insurance Friendship Heights, MD (Washington, DC area)	$30-$60/month in Garage $10/month in Lot	$30/month alternative mode subsidy; plus $0.051/mile for carpools	0.61	0.71	-14.1%
CH2M Hill Bellevue, WA, CBD	$60/month SOV $40/month carpool-2 $10/month carpool-3+	$40/month transportation allowance for all	0.55	0.90	-38.9%
City/County of Denver Denver CBD	Market parking rates only	misc. alternative mode subsidies	0.65	0.81	-19.3%
Bellevue City Hall Bellevue, WA (fringe)	$35/month SOV $17.50/month carpool	$39.50/month transit $39.50/month vanpool	0.63	0.90	-30.0%
Southern California Gas Los Angeles CBD	Graduated	$50/month transp. allowance $60 transit subsidy	0.41	0.78	-47.4%
US WEST Bellevue, WA, CBD	$60/month SOV $45/month carpool-2 $0/month carpool-3+	none	0.57	0.83	-31.3%
Swedish Hospital Seattle, WA, CBD (fringe)	$58/month SOV $5/month carpool plus $1 per passenger	$15/month transit	0.51	0.71	-28.2%
NOAA Silver Spring, MD, CBD	$65/month SOV and carpool-2 $30/month carpool-3+	$21/month transit	0.48	0.75	-36.0%
Nuclear Regulatory Commission Montgomery Co., MD (Suburban Strip)	$126/month SOV $60/month non-SOV	$21/month transit	0.59	0.85	-30.6%

Source: Comsis (1994), US WEST trip rate recalculation by Handbook authors (see case study, "US WEST Parking… Bellevue Washington").

In still another example, the city of Seattle reduced parking charges for carpools at two Seattle parking facilities downtown, from $25 to $5 per month at one facility and from $25 to nothing at the other. A survey of participants in the carpool incentive program reported that while the reduced parking charges stimulated new carpool formation, 40 percent of the participants were former bus riders and 38 percent already rideshared. Only 22 percent had switched from driving alone. This finding raised questions about the impact of the program on vehicle volumes and vehicle use in the downtown area. In addition, a significant number of participants were attracted from less convenient parking farther from the CBD (Olsson and Miller, 1978). This example is discussed further under "Travel Alternatives" in the "Underlying Traveler Response Factors" section.

UNDERLYING TRAVELER RESPONSE FACTORS

Several of the factors underlying traveler response to parking pricing have been alluded to in the presentation of impacts. This section examines in more detail the mechanisms by which the factors work.

Income

The value of travelers' time rises along with income. Higher-income travelers may be less sensitive to changes in prices for parking because parking is a smaller portion of their total income. Lower income travelers, on the other hand, are more likely to change behavior to avoid parking charges. This notion is lent support, albeit not empirical, by the following research:

Microsimulation modeling techniques were used with Census Public Use Microdata Sample (PUMS) data from Sacramento and Los Angeles to test the impact of parking policies on different income groups. The policies examined included a flat regional parking charge increment of five dollars per day, and also a core area parking charge of three dollars in the central core, two dollars in the peripheral core, and zero in suburban areas. Estimated results, as measured by impact on SOV work trips, are presented in Table 13-18. The results suggest that SOV use rates are initially lowest in the bottom income strata and that these groups also show the greatest proportional response to changes in parking price.

Parking Supply/Management

Institution of parking fees is more readily done in environments where the parking supply is limitedby either market or regulatory conditions. Availability of alternative parking options will limit the effectiveness of parking prices. As in the Chicago example, presented in the previous section under "Short- Versus Long-Term Differentials" — "Increase in Rate Differential," patrons of publicly operated garages may switch to private parking if price increases make the private garages more comparable. Likewise, employees may seek free off-site parking (often on-street parking) to avoid parking charges at work sites. Over the long run, there is a risk that parking pricing implemented in one area and not in surrounding areas may encourage a shift to destinations that do not charge for parking, or where rates are more favorable. Quantitative information on the degree of risk, i.e., the potential extent of shift, is currently lacking.

Table 13-18 Estimated Impacts of Parking Policy by Income Quintile in Sacramento and Los Angeles

	Income Quintile					
	1	2	3	4	5	Total
Baseline SOV work trip share						
Sacramento	0.65	0.71	0.76	0.79	0.77	0.75
Los Angeles	0.58	0.64	0.70	0.75	0.80	0.72
$5 regional fee (percent change in SOV work trip share)						
Sacramento	-43%	-26%	-15%	-10%	-8%	-16%
Los Angeles	-39%	-23%	-14%	-9%	-4%	-12%
Core parking fee (percent change in SOV work trip share)						
Sacramento	-14%	-8%	-5%	-3%	-2%	-5%
Los Angeles	-27%	-16%	-9%	-6%	-3%	-8%

Notes: Average regional values are presented here for estimated baseline SOV work trip mode share probabilities and percent changes. Note, however, that impacts were calculated to vary several fold across local areas within each region.

Source: Portland State University (1995).

Changes in the management of public parking and publicly provided incentives and transit alternatives can also affect the outcome of parking pricing. For example, a local agency might provide free shuttles to remote parking locations at the same time as downtown parking prices are raised, facilitating parking location shifts (perhaps to reduce core area congestion) at the expense of vehicle trip reduction. In the case of a parking tax, most of the increased price will be paid by consumers if the parking supply is tight and demand relatively inelastic. If the parking supply is plentiful, parking operators may tend to absorb more of the tax and thus face reduced income.

Worth pointing out is that public policy towards provision of parking supply is often at odds with the goals of parking pricing strategies. Local planning boards or zoning agencies often set *minimum* parking supply requirements for new developments, resulting in ubiquitous free parking that is difficult to price. For further discussion of parking supply/management issues, see Chapter 18, "Parking Management and Supply."

Land Use and Site Design

Parking pricing is much more likely to be successfully implemented in areas with favorable land use characteristics and site design. Design of the parking facilities themselves should enhance management and restriction for enforcement purposes. The setting should provide access to transit and to basic services that do not require a vehicle to reach, so that commuters are not made captive to their automobiles, either by the demands of their primary trip or for meeting incidental needs such as meals or banking.

TCRP Project B-4 found that the most successful commute trip reduction programs were located in suburban CBDs or in the regional CBD fringes, while the least effective programs were in isolated suburban, exurban and rural areas. Non-auto local area site accessibility, as measured by the number of services located within a five minute walk of each site, was likewise found to be significantly related to trip reduction: TDM sites with poor access to services had a vehicle trip rate that was 5.3 percent lower than ambient trip rates, the rate for sites with fair access was 8.3 percent lower and sites with good local area pedestrian access had a rate 21.5 percent lower than ambient (Comsis, 1994). Although logical on the face of it, it may be premature to read too much into the relationship, however. Sites that have good local area pedestrian access may on the whole be the same sites where densities facilitate higher parking prices, so that part of the differential may be a function of pricing.

Travel Alternatives

The degree to which parking pricing will be effective in trip reduction also depends upon the traveler's perception of the comparability and quality of available travel alternatives. If transit service is to be an effective substitute for driving, it must be direct enough and frequent enough to offer convenient access and competitive travel time, as well as being attractively priced. The same holds true for carpooling and vanpooling, where incentives in parking priority or preferential lanes or access can help offset inherent limitations in flexibility and travel time compared to driving alone. Employer subsidization of transit fares, carpool and vanpool parking, or other financial incentives can help balance the scales in making non-drive-alone modes competitive.

Table 13-19 provides one perspective on the interplay between parking charges, quality of alternative mode service, and traveler response, here in the specific case of transit service improvements. The relationships in Table 13-19 are model generated using augmented NPTS data for 20 consolidated metropolitan areas and produced by varying one parameter at a time. Comparison of the estimated mode shares gives an idea, subject to the limitations of the multi-city cross-sectional research model, of the relative importance of transit coverage (percent within 1/4 mile), amount and frequency of service (revenue hours per capita), and the likelihood that the traveler has to pay for parking (expressed as a probability) (Dueker, Strathman and Bianco, 1998). Note that data pairs representing a 100 percent increase for each attribute are highlighted with matched bold or italic figures in order to facilitate balanced comparison among attributes.

The NPTS-based analysis suggests that parking pricing is a more potent tool for decreasing SOV commutes than either enhancing transit access or increasing transit service levels (Dueker, Strathman and Bianco, 1998). Directly comparable information on the importance of carpooling characteristics is not available from this same study.

Relative importance of modal attributes is not the same as modal substitutability, of course. This has been addressed, for priced parking versus transit service, using a different research model. Sample enumeration techniques were employed, using the "STEP" model, to estimate work trip mode shares achievable with a flat $5 regionwide parking fee in each of five west coast metropolitan areas of varying sizes and transit service levels. The results were then used to relate percent reduction in SOV trips, with the $5 fee, to levels of transit service. The findings, displayed in Table 13-20, show the SOV trip reduction effects to be strongest in or near the core, in large cities, and where overall transit service levels are high, in that general order of importance.

Table 13-19   Predicted Mode Share for Alternative Levels of Transit Access, Transit Service, and "Pay-to-Park" Probability

Attribute/Level	Modal Shares		
	SOV	Carpool	Transit
(1) Percent within 1/4 mile of transit			
30	**0.785**	**0.129**	**0.086**
40	0.781	0.130	0.089
50	0.778	0.131	0.091
60	**0.775**	**0.132**	**0.093**
(2) Revenue Hours per Capita			
0.75	**0.806**	**0.141**	**0.053**
1.00	*0.800*	*0.138*	*0.062*
1.25	0.792	0.135	0.073
1.50	**0.782**	**0.132**	**0.086**
1.75	0.772	0.128	0.100
2.00	*0.760*	*0.125*	*0.115*
(3) Pay-to-Park Probability			
0.01	0.816	0.138	0.046
0.05	**0.771**	**0.131**	**0.098**
0.10	**0.674**	**0.121**	**0.205**
0.15	0.544	0.119	0.337

Notes: Model was developed from 1990 NPTS commute trip data. Attribute (1) represents percent of respondents living within a quarter mile of a transit stop, (2) represents a metropolitan area measure of transit frequency and coverage, and (3) represents likelihood that commuters pay for parking at work. The data pairs for each attribute that are highlighted with matched bold or italic figures identify 100 percent increases in the attribute.

Source: Dueker, Strathman and Bianco (1998).

Table 13-20   Estimated Percentage Reductions in SOV Work Trips in Response to $5-per-Day Regionwide Parking Charge, under Differing Conditions

	Percent Reduction in SOV Trips					
Size of Metro Area	Small City			Large City		
Location of Trip-Maker's Residence	Urban Core	Near Core	Suburb	Urban Core	Near Core	Suburb
Level of Transit Service						
High	25%	19%	12%	36%	26%	14%
Medium	23	17	11	32	23	13
Low	20	15	10	29	21	11

Source: Dueker, Strathman and Bianco (1998).

The estimated SOV trip reduction varies from 10 percent where transit would be poorest (suburbs of small cities with low levels of overall transit service) to 36 percent where transit would be best (core areas of large cities with high levels of overall transit service). The researchers note that in addition to transit, carpooling captures some of the trips dissuaded from SOV commuting. They conclude that the amount diverted to carpooling is inversely related to the level of transit service available (Dueker, Strathman and Bianco, 1998).

Still another perspective on the role of travel alternatives, this time in the specific case of ridesharing incentives, is offered by a 1978 evaluation of carpool parking discounts. In 1975-76, Seattle's Commuter Pool agency introduced reduced-rate parking at two city-owned parking facilities on the fringe of the CBD. The evaluation of the impact of the parking discount program on carpool formation was done via a survey of 113 carpool lot users in 1977. Key findings are summarized in Table 13-21.

Table 13-21   Seattle Pool Parking Discount Experiment Mode Shift Analysis

Parameter	Former Mode of Observed Carpoolers		
	Drove Alone	Transit	Carpool
Percent of carpoolers from indicated prior mode	22%	40%	38%
Average trip length (miles)	13.4	9.8	14.3
Percent reporting shifting of modes because of:			
Parking discount	20%	15%	19%
Money savings	80	38	42
Time savings	12	29	34
Convenience	52	44	60
Percent reporting time savings over previous mode/commute	38%	82%	16%
Percent of former "Drive Alones" who previously paid for parking	75%	–	–
Percent of former "Drive Alones" reporting time savings who previously had free parking	100%	–	–
Percent of former "Drive Alones" now closer to downtown destination	44%	–	–
Carpool mode longevity – months carpooling	25 mos.	15 mos.	75 mos.
Prior carpool occupancy of prior "Carpoolers"	–	–	3.5
New carpool occupancy of prior "Carpoolers" with discounted parking	–	–	3.8
Demographics:			
Professional/Managerial	60%	51%	63%
Male	72%	56%	66%
Autos per driver in the household	0.94	0.85	0.82

Source: Olsson and Miller (1978).

In the Seattle experiment, the parking rate of $25 per month at one facility was eliminated entirely for pools of 3 or more persons and discounted to $5 per month at the other. Additional incentives for carpooling independent of the discounted parking were also being offered in the area at about the same time, including opening a bus priority lane to carpools, cutting an associated bridge toll from 19¢ to 10¢, opening a priority ramp to the I-5 freeway, and conducting an areawide matching and promotional program. While not attempting to account for the role of the other carpool incentives, the evaluation results suggest that (Olsson and Miller, 1978):

- Two out of every five pool units or equivalent were in place before the discount experiment.

- New pool users had shorter trip lengths than former pool users.

- Two out of five new carpool users were former transit users, shifting primarily because of time or money savings, or convenience. Time savings were reported by 82 percent of former transit users.

- One out of five new carpool users was a former Drive Alone commuter, 75 percent of whom had paid for parking.

  - Of the 25 percent who formerly had free parking, all reported time savings as a result of the shift.

  - Of all with Drive Alone as their prior mode, 44 percent were able to park closer to their downtown destinations.

- Auto occupancy for those who pooled prior to the discount increased from 3.5 to 3.8. Only 6 out of 42 former pool units reported an occupancy decrease.

- The average life of carpool units (noting that the assessment was done 3 years after implementation of the discount) displayed a fairly significant pattern and lifespan:

  - Carpools with former solo drivers averaged over 2 years together.

  - Carpools with former transit users had little more than 1 year together.

  - Pre-discount carpool units had been together an average of 6-1/4 years.

- The facility with entirely free carpool parking was much more heavily utilized than the one with the $5 per month rate.

The Seattle analysis demonstrates empirically that a variety of mode shifts must be reckoned with when using parking pricing as an incentive and that shifting among travel modes can be fairly fluid when all primary options (drive alone, ridesharing and transit) are relatively competitive. The analysis and other experiences also suggest that when pricing and other incentives are used to encourage carpooling in an environment of competitive transit service, a majority of new carpoolers may well come from transit, although shifts from SOVs remain significant.

Other Incentives, Options, and Associated Programs

Most parking pricing initiatives, particularly those with any TDM orientation, are implemented in conjunction with a broader array of changes including improvements in transit service and various financial or compensatory incentives. It is important to note and be aware of these overlapping and potentially confounding circumstances. Table 13-22 provides additional case study examples illustrating the interplay of site setting, additional incentives and programs, and parking pricing for different types and sizes of employers. Table 13-22 is based on "with and without" analysis that compares individual TDM program sites with ambient conditions, in other words, overall averages for the surrounding immediate area (Comsis, 1994). Additional information of this type – with accompanying interpretation and data extending into the early 2000s – is found in Chapter 19, "Employer and Institutional TDM Strategies."

Short-Term Versus Long-Term Response

A travel behavior question that may be leveled at all strategies is that of the permanence or duration of a particular change in behavior. In the short term, there may be a lag in response to disincentive strategies such as parking price increases, while alternatives are explored and travel arrangements made. In the medium term, travelers may be expected to exhibit the greatest mode choice response, particularly if their opportunities to circumvent the change are limited. For travelers such as commuters or students who are locked into a pattern of regular visitation to a particular site, the choice when faced with new or increased parking costs is either to pay the fee or to switch modes. Non-work travelers presumably have more choice in where they travel and how often, and therefore, may not be as likely to switch modes.

In the longer run, some households, workers, businesses and organizations might be expected to shift the locations of their origins or destinations to avoid the strategy's effect and reestablish their previous modal choices. However, much depends on how broadly the strategy has been implemented in the area, and what alternatives or other amenities exist to offset the disutility of the parking fee. For example, continuing to work in a busy CBD may have other benefits to balance the lack of free parking. Such benefits may range from transportation advantages, like the ability to rely on rail or bus rapid transit, or business or social benefits, such as opportunities for diverse professional or personal interactions.

Retention over time of travel behavior changes made in response to a system change or strategy has not been well studied in the case of parking pricing. Evidence from TDM studies, however, suggests that programs which are based on well-conceived and balanced cost incentive/disincentive actions and offer realistic alternatives to travelers tend to have visibly greater effect on employee vehicle trip rates and tend to better sustain their effects over time. These more favorable outcomes are in marked contrast to TDM programs that feature only "soft" incentives and support measures, and pertain both to cases where parking is constrained and thus inherently supportive of pricing, and to cases where the priced parking is largely or entirely attributable to regulatory requirements for trip reduction (Comsis and Katz Associates, 1990; Comsis, 1994).

TCRP Project B-4 investigated 49 employer TDM programs, and took note of changes in program measures and traveler responses over time. It found that programs with priced and managed parking at their core required far fewer program changes, in terms of new or additional strategies, as employers sought to effectively address regulatory or other needs to reduce employee vehicle trip rates and then maintain the reductions (Comsis, 1994).

Table 13-22 Relationship Between Parking Pricing and/or Subsidies and Vehicle Trip Rates at Employment Sites

Type Employer and Site	Setting	Employment	Parking Pricing	Subsidies	Vehicle Trip Rate *per capita*	Ambient Trip Rate *per capita*	Site versus Ambient Trip Rate
Professional/Office							
Prudential	CBD	3,400	None	None	0.82	0.87	-5.7%
Aetna	CBD	2,450	None	$21/mo. Transit	0.77	0.77	Same
Hartford Steam Boiler	CBD	300	$110/mo. SOV $75/mo. CP-2 $40/mo. CP-3 $10/mo. CP-4+	50% Transit Subsidy	0.49	0.77	-36.4%
Payroll One	Suburban CBD	21	None	None	0.80	0.81	-1.2%
GEICO	Suburban CBD	2,100	$30-$60/mo. in Garage $10/mo. in Lot	$30/mo. Alternative Mode Subsidies +$0.051/mile for Carpools	0.61	0.71	-14.1%
CH2M Hill	Suburban CBD	400	$60/mo. SOV $40/mo. CP-2 $10/mo. CP-3+	$40/mo. Transportation Allowance for All	0.55	0.90	-38.9%
Dean-Witter	Office Park	1,700	None	Alt. Mode Subsidy ($??)	0.88	0.93	-5.4%
Chubb Insurance	Office Park	1,300	None	None	0.87	0.92	-5.4%
Rick Engineering	Office Park	120	None	$25/mo. Alt. Modes	0.77	0.85	-9.4%
Commercial/Service							
City Place Mall	Suburban CBD	320	$65/mo.	$21/mo. Transit	0.55	0.75	-26.2%
K-Mart Valencia	Strip Mall	112	None	None	0.91	0.87	+4.6%
G-Street Fabrics	Strip Mall	200	None	$11/mo. Transit	0.75	0.85	-11.8%
Mercy Home Care	Office Park	270	None	None	0.90	0.85	+5.6%
Warner Center Hilton	Office Park	165	None	$15/mo. Alt. Modes	0.49	0.87	-43.7%

Table 13-22   Relationship Between Parking Pricing and/or Subsidies and Vehicle Trip Rates at Employment Sites (continued)

Type Employer and Site	Setting	Employ-ment	Parking Pricing	Subsidies	Vehicle Trip Rate *per capita*	Ambient Trip Rate *per capita*	Site versus Ambient Trip Rate
Manufacturing/Industrial							
Allergan	Office Park	1,400	None	100% Vanpool Subsidy 50% Transit Subsidy	0.75	0.87	-13.8%
P.L. Porter	Suburban Campus	230	None	$15/mo. Transit	0.67	0.87	-23.0%
Nike	Suburban Campus	2,200	None	50% Transit Subsidy $1/day all Others	0.83	0.88	-5.7%
Boeing Corp.	8 Sites	85,000	None	$15/mo. Transit	0.80	0.89	-10.1%
Rockbestos	Exurban	400	None	None	0.66	0.93	-29.0%
Sears	Exurban	5,400	None	$80/mo. Alt. Modes	0.53	0.92	-42.4%
Shure Brothers	Exurban	500	None	None	0.81	0.81	Same
Master Magnetics	Exurban	50	None	None	0.86	0.93	-5.4%
Hewlett-Packard	Exurban	3,000	None	None	0.86	0.91	-5.5%
Hughes Aircraft	Exurban	5,000	None	None	0.75	0.87	-14.0%
Municipalities							
Hillsboro Co., FL	CBD	2,050	None	$21/mo. Transit $16/mo. Vanpool	0.85	0.88	-3.4%
City/County of Denver	CBD	12,000	None	Misc. Alt. Mode Subsidy	0.65	0.81	-19.3%
City of Pleasanton, CA	Suburban CBD	360	None	25% TR & VP Subsidy $1.50/day Alternative Mode "Bonus"	0.84	0.89	-5.6%
Pasadena City Hall	Sub'n. CBD	2,000	$35/mo. SOV	$35/mo. Transit	0.66	0.81	-18.5%
Arlington Hts., IL	Suburban CBD	250	None	Up to $42/mo. for Alternative Modes	0.80	0.91	-12.1%
Bellevue City Hall	Office Park	650	$35/mo. SOV $17.50/mo CP	$39.50/mo. Transit $39.50/mo. VP	0.63	0.90	-30.0%

Table 13-22 Relationship Between Parking Pricing and/or Subsidies and Vehicle Trip Rates at Employment Sites (continued)

Type Employer and Site	Setting	Employment	Parking Pricing	Subsidies	Vehicle Trip Rate *per capita*	Ambient Trip Rate *per capita*	Site vs. Ambient Trip Rate
Utility							
Southern Calif. Gas	CBD	1,800	Graduated	$50/mo. Transportation Allowance $60 Transit Subsidy	0.41	0.78	-47.4%
Georgia Power	CBD	1,800	$10/mo. SOV & CP-2 $0 for CP-3+	Transit Subsidy ($??)	0.91	0.79	+15.1%
US WEST	Suburban CBD	1,100	$65/mo. SOV $45/mo CP-2 $0/mo. CP-3+	None	0.57	0.83	-31.3%
AT&T	Suburban CBD	950	$65/mo.	$21/mo. Transit	0.57	0.75	-24.0%
GTE Systems	Office Park	1,350	None	Transit Subsidy ($??)	0.94	0.91	+3.3%
Medical Institution							
Cedars Sinai Hospital	CBD Fringe	6,000	None	Alt. Mode Cash Out $15/mo. Transit	0.76	0.87	-12.6%
Swedish Hospital	CBD Fringe	2,250	$58/mo. SOV $5/mo. CP plus $1 per passenger	$15/mo. Transit	0.51	0.71	-28.2%
Boulder Hospital	CBD Fringe	1,000	None	$4/day Alternative Modes	0.67	0.78	-14.1%
Washington Adventist	Suburban Campus	1,800	None	$11/mo. Transit	0.80	0.71	+12.6%
Baxter Healthcare	Exurban	1,000	None	$60/mo. Alt. Modes	0.93	0.90	+3.3%

Table 13-22 Relationship Between Parking Pricing and/or Subsidies and Vehicle Trip Rates at Employment Sites (continued)

Type Employer and Site	Setting	Employ-ment	Parking Pricing	Subsidies	Vehicle Trip Rate *per capita*	Ambient Trip Rate *per capita*	Site versus Ambient Trip Rate
Educational Institution							
Univ. Central Florida	Suburban Campus	5,000	None	None	0.96	0.86	+11.6%
Cornell University	Suburban Campus	10,900	$?? for SOV	100% Transit Subsidy	0.72	0.83	-13.2%
Univ. of Washington	Suburban Campus	17,400	$36/mo. Staff $4/day Students $0 for Carpools	$40/mo. Transit	0.27	0.71	-62.0%
Other Institutional							
NOAA	Suburban CBD	5,000	$65/mo. SOV & CP-2 $30/mo. CP-3+	$21/mo. Transit	0.48	0.75	-36.0%
Nuclear Regulatory Commission	Suburban Strip	1,400	$126/mo. SOV $60/mo. non-SOV	$21/mo. Transit	0.59	0.85	-30.6%
California Tax Board	Office Park	4,600	None	$15 Transit Subsidy $50 VP *Driver* Subsidy	0.84	0.89	-5.6%
Nat. Optical Observat.	Suburban Campus	250	None	50% Transit Subsidy	0.50	0.83	-39.8%
Lawrence Livermore	Exurban	9,300	None	$20 Transit Subsidy	0.71	0.86	-17.4%
McLellan AFB	Military Base	12,000	None	None	0.97	0.89	+9.0%

Notes: CP = Carpool, TR = Transit, VP = Vanpool, ?? = Specific amount not known

Sources: Comsis (1994), US WEST trip rate recalculation by Handbook authors as described in and per sources of the case study, "US WEST Parking Pricing and Management – Bellevue, Washington."

RELATED INFORMATION AND IMPACTS

Mode and Destination Shifts

Proponents of parking pricing schemes may assume that reduction in parking demand will occur entirely through mode shifts rather than in part through reduced trip making or activity at a parking destination. Yet, with the exception of commuters, most travelers do have a choice of destinations for their activities. Unless acceptable travel alternatives are available, they may well switch destinations.

Various examples of the mode shares that do accompany parking pricing are provided in the preceding sections of this chapter, shown either as mode shifts (before and after shares) or as comparative mode shares under different parking pricing scenarios. For empirical findings covering mode shifts or mode share comparisons, with at least three-way (SOV, carpool, transit) breakouts, refer in particular to Tables 13-3, 13-11, 13-12 and 13-13 within the "Response by Type of Strategy" section.

Differential parking fees, as well as other incentives and options, can influence the modes to which travel demand shifts. If rideshare vehicles are given free parking, for example, former solo drivers are more likely to carpool than to use transit, and even transit users may be persuaded to carpool. The Seattle discounted carpool parking program – discussed within the "Underlying Traveler Response Factors" section in connection with Table 13-21 – is a good example of this, having drawn 40 percent of its participants from transit versus only 22 percent from SOVs (Olsson and Miller, 1978). If subsidized transit passes are provided while rideshare vehicles pay for parking, the opposite is likely to be true.

Cost Effectiveness

Since parking is a commodity that is often not priced, introducing parking charges at a site or in a subarea, or even imposing a tax or alternative fee structure, will involve various additional costs to the implementing agency or company. The question thus raised is whether the costs incurred are exceeded by the revenues (or other benefits) associated with the pricing and management of parking supply. Costs to run a parking program include any capital or up-front planning and implementation costs, ongoing administrative and operating costs, and enforcement costs where applicable.

Because parking demand typically has been shown to be inelastic with respect to price, imposition of or increases in parking fees are generally met with increases in total revenue. However, to the extent that there are readily available substitutes – such as free employer off-site parking, on-street parking, or reasonably priced alternative parking facilities – the demand response may be greater than the typical -0.3 elasticity suggests. The response may even tend toward an elastic response. A good example is the Chicago case that was illustrated in Table 13-6. In most cases, however, an increase in parking fees should result in a revenue increase that covers the costs, and hence should be a "cost-effective" action.

There are a couple of notable twists, however. First, as in the case of the San Francisco parking tax, raising fees through introduction of a parking surcharge may produce an increase in total revenue overall, but for the facility operator *whose own rate is unchanged while total fee increases,* the decline in demand may well mean a net loss in revenue to the operator. Thus the question becomes: "Cost effective to whom?"

The other important twist on cost effectiveness of parking pricing relates to what costs (or benefits) are included in the assessment. If parking pricing results in changes in travel behavior that address a policy objective, such as reduction in VMT (and correspondingly, traffic congestion or air pollution), these benefits become an important *societal* component of the cost effectiveness determination. Private benefits and costs may also be favorably affected by broader definition of cost effectiveness. For example, a reduction in vehicle parking demand may result in cost *savings*, particularly to building owners or employers who might otherwise be required by code or market pressures to supply a given quantity of parking. Imposing or raising parking fees in situations where the owner is able to avoid or divest of site parking may offer a two part benefit: earning revenues in excess of costs by levying a parking fee, and obtaining savings for that parking capacity they avoid having to provide.

An illustration of this broader definition of cost-effectiveness is offered by the data in Table 13-23, drawn from the research of TCRP Project B-4, "Cost Effectiveness of Travel Demand Management (TDM) Strategies." The table shows various cost/performance measures calculated by level of employee parking fee, which has been categorized as "free," "nominal," or "market." Program cost information was processed along with information on the size of the employment base, credited employee vehicle trip reduction, and parking conditions and costs, in order to produce the performance measures defined as follows:

- Annual Direct Cost per Employee: Total annualized cost of implementing and administering program, less any offsetting revenues (especially from parking fees).

- Annual Net Cost per Employee: Direct costs as described, but further reduced by any indirect benefits experienced or costs avoided (in this case exclusively costs related to supplying parking that the employer could actually avoid through divestiture).

- Direct Cost per Daily Trip Reduced: Places the annual direct cost in relation to the actual number of vehicle trips reduced on a *daily* basis.

- Net Cost per Daily Trip Reduced: As above, but with the direct costs reduced by the amount of benefits experienced or costs avoided.

The data show a fairly strong relationship between the type of parking pricing and the direct and net cost performance of the TDM program to the employer. Programs where parking is free to employees cost employers an average of $37.74 a year per employee, and $2.03 per daily trip reduced. Contrast this with only $12.61 per employee and $0.50 per trip reduced for programs where parking carries a nominal charge, and an actual savings of $50.04 per employee and $0.96 per daily trip reduced for those programs with parking priced at market rates.

When the employer TDM program costs are further reduced by introducing an estimate of the cost savings that might be attributed to parking liabilities foregone, then the annual *Net Cost* per employee or per trip looks even more attractive to the employer who charges for parking. Table 13-23 shows a net cost for sites with free parking that is $28.70 per employee, and $1.76 per daily trip reduced. This is both because the trip demand was not greatly reduced in these programs, and because the employer probably could not reduce its parking infrastructure.

However, in cases where employees experience a charge for parking, the net costs per trip or employee are negative, representing employer savings, both because of sizable trip reductions and because the employer can realistically divest itself of its excess parking obligations. When these savings are accounted for, the programs with "nominal" parking charges show a net annual savings of $152.49 per employee and $3.72 per daily trip reduced. Where parking is priced at "market rates," the savings are higher: $236 per year per employee and $3.76 per daily trip reduced.

Table 13-23   Average Employer Cost of TDM Programs by Level of Parking Fee

Parking Fees Experienced by Employees	Annual Direct Cost per Employee	Direct Cost per Daily Trip Reduced	Annual Net Cost per Employee	Net Cost per Daily Trip Reduced
Free	$37.74	$2.03	$28.70	$1.76
Nominal	12.61	0.50	-152.49	-3.72
Market	-50.04	-0.96	-236.02	-3.76
All	$14.70	$0.75	-$62.30	-$0.78

Source: Comsis (1994). From survey of 49 employer TDM programs.

Beyond the conclusions implied by the TCRP Project B-4 data, a growing body of literature suggests that if the objective of a TDM program is to promote transit use and ridesharing, then it is more cost effective to eliminate parking subsidies to solo drivers than to offer additional subsidies to transit users and ridesharers while continuing to subsidize drive-alone parking (Mehranian et al, 1987).

Parking pricing has various advantages and disadvantages as a traffic mitigation and emissions reduction strategy. It must be well thought through and executed to be effective and avoid unintended consequences. Many of the issues and concerns are parallel to those of parking supply management. Those considerations are examined in the "Environmental Relationships" and "Critical Aspects of Parking Supply Management" subsections of Chapter 18, "Parking Management and Supply," in that chapter's "Related Information and Impacts Section." Additional issues are closely tied with those of other TDM strategies and are addressed in Chapter 19, "Employer and Institutional TDM Strategies." Already, here in Chapter 13, it is extensively documented that parking pricing as a TDM strategy is closely associated with effective, durable TDM programs (see especially "Elimination of Employer Parking Subsidy" in the "Response by Type of Strategy" section, and "Short-Term Versus Long-Term Response" in the "Underlying Traveler Response Factors" section).

Parking pricing will be most effective as an environmental strategy if a large proportion of the parking supply is priced. Otherwise, travelers may be able to avoid the fees by traveling elsewhere, possibly at greater distance. Even broad parking pricing strategies cannot be ubiquitous by time of day and location the way that congestion pricing has the potential to be, and in particular, cannot address through traffic (Metro and Oregon DOT, 2000).

Reductions in emissions may be estimated based on the changes in vehicle trips and VMT induced by parking pricing. Table 13-24 provides an example of the kinds of emissions reductions that might be expected at an employment site upon institution of parking pricing. An example of predicted fuel consumption effects was provided earlier in Table 13-14 and estimated regional emissions reductions for employee parking pricing – based on travel demand and air quality modeling – were provided for California regions in Table 13-15, both in the "Elimination of Employer Parking Subsidy" subsection.

Table 13-24 Summary of Parking Cash-Out Emissions and Fuel Consumption Impacts

Measure	Change (per Employee per Year)	Percent Change
Vehicle Trips	-43	-11%
Vehicle Miles Traveled (VMT)	-652	-12%
Reactive Organic Gases (lb.)	-1.8	-12%
Nitrogen Oxides (lb.)	-1.5	-12%
Carbon Monoxide (lb.)	-15.9	-12%
Particulate Matter (lb.)	-1.1	-12%
Carbon Dioxide (lb.)	-514	-12%
Gasoline Consumption (gallons)	-26	-12%

Notes: Emissions reductions estimated based on reductions in vehicle trips and VMT using the California Air Resource Board's EMFAC7F1.1/B7F model.

Source: Average values for eight employment site case studies reported in Shoup (1997).

ADDITIONAL RESOURCES

TCRP Report 40, "Strategies to Attract Auto Users to Public Transportation" (Dueker, Strathman and Bianco, 1998), examines the effectiveness of parking pricing strategies for increasing transit ridership. Travel mode choice and other impacts are estimated for eight strategies involving transit service levels and the price and availability of parking, alone and in combination. The final chapter is an implementation guide for transportation planners and decisionmakers.

Evaluating the Effects of Parking Cash Out: Eight Case Studies, prepared for the California Air Resources Board (Shoup, 1997), is one of a series of studies and papers by the author on the effects of parking pricing, employer-subsidized parking, and California's Parking Cash-Out Program. It includes extensive information on how eight employers implemented parking cash-out, each approach customized to the particular needs of the employer, along with quantitative analysis of the effects on parking demand, mode choice, trip rates, VMT and emissions.

Analysis of the Potential Effectiveness of Parking Pricing Based Transportation Control Measures Using Stated Response Data, University of South Florida (Kuppam, Pendyala and Gollakoti, 1997), offers an alternative approach to evaluating response of travelers to parking pricing. It focuses on employer vouchers as an alternative to subsidized parking and the use of a stated response methodology to examine courses of action commuters might choose to take.

The Victoria Transport Policy Institute (VTPI) maintains an "Online TDM Encyclopedia" http://www.vtpi.org/tdm/. This online compendium offers information on a broad range of TDM strategies and includes the web documents "Parking Pricing" and "Transportation Elasticities" (with elasticities for parking pricing). The periodically updated coverage includes encapsulated travel demand response observation and estimates along with references and leads to more information (Victoria Transport Policy Institute, 2003). In addition an "ITE Parking Management Report" is under preparation for the ITE Parking Council by Todd Litman of VTPI.

CASE STUDIES

A Parking Tax in the City of San Francisco

Situation. For almost two years beginning in October 1970, the city and county of San Francisco imposed a 25 percent *ad valorem* tax on parking within its jurisdiction. This action was taken for the express purpose of raising revenue in lieu of a more general property tax levy. There was no stated policy purpose accompanying the parking tax, such as traffic, energy, or environmental management. However, the magnitude of the parking price change introduced by the tax (at that time, the largest city-wide jump in parking prices in history), coupled with the large area over which the pricing change was felt, provides important insights for those contemplating use of parking fees or taxes as a way of achieving travel changes.

Actions. The parking tax was levied on October 1, 1970, in the form of a 25 percent tax on all public and private off-street parking with the exception of residential spaces. The 49,614 off-street spaces affected by the tax included 22,328 garage spaces (92.8 percent of which were municipal, i.e., operated under agreement with the government) and 26,386 spaces in surface lots (70.5 percent municipal). The 11,172 on-street parking spaces in the city, of which 4,951 were metered, were unaffected by the tax. The tax was reduced to 10 percent on July 1, 1972, in response to continued opposition from affected individuals and business interests.

Analysis. Using *ex post facto* data compiled by 13 municipal garages (total of 9,496 spaces) before and throughout the period of the tax-induced parking price changes, elasticities were calculated in relation to changes in number of cars parked and normalized gross revenues. Formal analysis was limited to the municipal garages because of 1) availability of consistent data, compiled as part of their operation under city management, and 2) assurance that the full increment of the tax was reflected in the eventual parking fee. Private parking operators were known to have absorbed some of the tax burden themselves in order to lessen the impact on customers.

Parking price elasticities were calculated using the log-arc formulation on the basis of both number of cars parked and gross revenue. Separate computations were performed for 1) the initial period of 25 percent increase, and 2) the period during which the tax was dropped from 25 percent to 10 percent. Separate elasticities were also calculated for 1) facilities primarily used by commuters and 2) facilities oriented more to shoppers and recreational users. Also, because in the years prior to the tax levy parking demand and gross revenues had been steadily increasing (2.8 percent annually in number of cars parked, and 4.9 percent annually in gross income), the elasticity computations were adjusted to discount this "secular" growth. Exogenous factors that were acknowledged to have potentially affected use of parking and therefore the tax impact analysis included increased central area congestion caused by construction of the Bay Area Rapid Transit (BART) system, increased fares on the San Francisco Municipal Railway, and greatly improved transit services to suburban areas north of the Golden Gate.

Results. Estimated parking price elasticities based on the number of cars parked averaged -0.20 for FY 1970-71, the initial year of the tax (calculated vis-à-vis the pre-tax period FY 1969-70), and -0.31 for FY 1971-72 (vis-à-vis 1969-70). An elasticity of -0.38 was calculated for FY 1972-73, the year that the tax rate was *dropped* from 25 percent to 10 percent (calculated vis-à-vis 1971-72). These elasticities were seen as supporting the conventional wisdom that parking demand is very inelastic.

When the impact of the tax on changes in parking revenues was estimated, however, a very different picture was painted. Parking price elasticities computed on the basis of normalized gross revenues (rather than number of cars parked) were found to be -1.44, -1.63, and -1.63, respectively, for the same three periods cited above. These results reflect an *elastic* response of parking demand with respect to changes in price, leading to a quite different conclusion as to the impact of a change in parking price, and providing better agreement with the observed behavior of the parking facility operators. The study author reasons that if parking operators truly believed parking demand to be inelastic, the market would cause rates to rise until total net revenue was maximized. He concludes that parking spaces are a unique type of rental commodity, since they can be purchased in quantities from several minutes to an entire day or more, and the price varies with the quantity of parking "time" purchased. Thus, parking rate increases may cause two types of responses: 1) a discontinuance of parking at the facility (possibly involving a shift to a substitute facility), or 2) a shortening of the term of occupancy.

Supporting this hypothesis, a notable difference was discovered in the price elasticity demonstrated by commuters versus shoppers and recreational users. As illustrated in Table 13-25, the initial year of the program appeared to show commuters reacting with considerably more sensitivity to the parking tax than shoppers, with a parking demand elasticity of -0.27 (versus -0.08 for shoppers) in FY 1970-71. The same relationship held in FY 1972-73 when the tax rate was lowered to 10 percent, reflected by elasticities of -0.91 versus -0.23. This result is contrary to what one commonly sees in travel demand studies and model coefficients. Non-work purpose travelers are normally found in such analyses to be *more* sensitive to price changes than work purpose travelers, ostensibly because non-work trips are discretionary, and hence can be made at another time, to another place, or less frequently (if at all).

However, if one looks at the elasticities for Gross Income (change in parking revenue with respect to parking price), they are both elastic and more comparable between commuter and shopper garages. In fact, in FY 1970-71, when the elasticity of autos parked to change in price was only -0.08 for shopper-oriented garages, the gross income elasticity was -1.23, suggesting that the impact on revenue was about 15 times more than on the change in number of autos parked. These findings were taken to indicate that commuters were more likely to discontinue parking in municipal properties altogether, while shoppers would simply reduce the amount of time that they would park rather than forego the trip entirely.

More... The study also uncovered information that showed that price elasticities at municipal surface lots affected by the parking tax were higher than for the garages, averaging -0.82 for a sample of 30 lots (based on autos parked). Ten privately-operated self-park lots showed a revenue-based elasticity of -1.72, while 8 lots of another private operation averaged -2.23. The more elastic nature of demand to price changes in these cases was reasoned to be more related to location of the facility than type of facility, since the garages were centrally located while the lots were further out from the activity areas.

Table 13-25   Parking Price Elasticities by Year of Tax Adjustment and Type of Garage

Year	Basis of Estimate	Commuter Garages	Shopper Garages
FY 1970-71	Autos Parked	-0.27	-0.08
	Gross Income	-1.50	-1.23
FY 1971-72	Autos Parked	-0.26	-0.25
	Gross Income	-1.29	-1.22
FY 1972-73	Autos Parked	-0.91	-0.23
	Gross Income	-2.19	-1.45
3 Year Average	Autos Parked	-0.48	-0.19
	Gross Income	-1.66	-1.30

When the parking tax was reduced from 25 percent to 10 percent in 1972, the response of commuters reflected much more sensitivity than when the tax was initially imposed. The drop in price meant that the demand for commuter-oriented parking increased in an almost elastic (-0.91) relationship, and gross income from parking revenues showed an elasticity of -2.19. The response at garages oriented to shoppers, meanwhile, was much less, with an elasticity for autos parked of only -0.23, and a gross income elasticity of -1.45. This suggests a gentle moderation back to more hours parked for shoppers, most of whom had not stopped parking at the facilities even during the steepest part of the rate hike.

Net revenues for the parking operators, under the full parking tax, were estimated to have fallen 36 percent below the level projected under normal growth. These losses exceeded somewhat the revenues that the municipal government collected from the tax and posed a serious question about the fairness of the tax. The growth of traffic crossing the Golden Gate Bridge slowed, and peak-period traffic volume growth was halted during the study period, but the contribution of the parking tax to these events was thought to be minimal. Similarly, retail sales at downtown department stores fell substantially during the first 9 months of the parking tax, yet the timing of the subsequent recovery and the long-term trend of downtown sales losses to suburban retailers suggested that the tax impact was probably inconsequential.

Source: Kulash, D., *Parking Taxes as Roadway Prices: A Case Study of the San Francisco Experience.* The Urban Institute, Paper 1212-9, Washington, DC (1974).

Madison Peak-Period Parking Pricing Demonstration

Situation. This 1980-81 demonstration project involved a peak-period charge levied at municipally-controlled parking facilities in Madison, Wisconsin. Application of the peak-period charge was preceded by various changes and implemented in concert with transit subsidies and provision of shuttles to fringe parking lots. The objective of the pricing and operational changes was to discourage automobile commute trips to the CBD in order to make parking for shopping and midday business trips more readily available.

Actions. The demonstration was implemented in four phases. First, all four municipal parking ramps and one of the parking lots were converted from various combinations of short-, medium-, and long-term parking to attendant operation. The parking spaces involved in this first phase represented approximately 76 percent of the off-street parking controlled by the city or 10.6 percent of the total parking supply. In the second phase, monthly transit passes were sold at a 75 percent discount to employees in the CBD. In the third phase, a shuttle service began serving three fringe parking lots. The second and third phases of the demonstration were instituted about one year and one month before the fourth phase, respectively. In the fourth phase, all parkers entering three of the municipal facilities between the hours of 7:00 AM and 9:30 AM and parking for more than three hours were assessed a $1.00 peak-period parking charge. Over 1,000 parking spaces representing about 22 percent of the public off-street parking supply were subject to this peak-period surcharge.

Analysis. The demonstration was evaluated using data from before-and-after parking surveys, a panel of commuters using the parking facilities subject to the peak-period charge, a control panel of commuters using non-surcharge parking facilities, and standard occupancy and duration counts.

Results. An immediate effect on the occupancy of parking facilities was observed after imposition of the peak-period charge. Occupancies at 9:00 AM declined on average by 40 percent at the three peak-period charge facilities. Occupancies at two nearby facilities not subject to the surcharge increased by about 80 cars per day and only the fact that these facilities filled to capacity by 9:00 AM prevented further increases in usage. By midday, occupancies at the surcharged facilities had increased to levels only about 7 percent below what they had been before the peak-period charge.

Prior to the surcharge, the shuttle bus to the fringe lots carried about 330 persons (660 one-way trips) per day. The surcharge was found to increase shuttle bus usage by only about 13 persons per day once the effect of a 10¢ bus fare increase was taken into account.

The panel of peak-period commuters who used the surcharged facilities prior to institution of the peak-period charge was compared to the panel who used non-surcharged parking facilities. The commuters facing the peak-period charge were found to be more likely to have switched parking locations and to have increased their use of transit and walking. These commuters were also more likely to have delayed their time of entry to the facilities to avoid the surcharge. Relatively few switched to one of the fringe parking facilities in response to the surcharge. The surcharge was also found to have relatively little influence on carpooling behavior. While a number of individuals changed carpool behavior after the surcharge was imposed, only a quarter of the panel who increased their vehicle occupancies attributed this change to the surcharge.

More... Perceptions of parking availability during the morning and midday periods improved significantly after imposition of the surcharge. This finding, combined with the changes in occupancy observed, suggest that the objectives of the demonstration program were met. The peak-period surcharge was in effect for about one year. After the surcharge was discontinued, parking rates were increased from 20¢ up to 35¢ per hour.

Source: Charles River Associates, Inc., "Madison Peak-Period Parking Pricing Demonstration Project." Urban Mass Transit Administration, Washington, DC (1984).

US WEST Parking Pricing and Management - Bellevue, Washington

Situation. Bellevue, Washington, is a suburb located about 5 miles east of Seattle, across Lake Washington. The Bellevue CBD, however, features densities and a street network more like a "traditional" downtown. CBD employment was over 24,000 in 1988. In addition to capital improvements, the city of Bellevue has attempted to mitigate congestion by requiring TDM plans from developers of new buildings; enhancing regular, express, and park-and-ride bus routes; and forming a Transportation Management Association (TMA) with broad functions including administration of a parking rental/management system. Parking for new buildings was limited by the city of Bellevue at the time to 2.7 spaces per 1,000 square feet of net usable space, with a minimum of 2.0 per 1,000 (as compared to the pre-1979 minimum of 5.0 per 1,000). US WEST, in relocating its headquarters to downtown Bellevue, chose to limit its supply of employee parking to 2.4 spaces per 1,000 square feet. US WEST agreed to make its building access-friendly to transit and pedestrians, another requirement of the city, and to implement a strategy for minimizing employee vehicle trips. A key part of the company's strategy was to strategically price and manage the limited employee parking.

Actions. US WEST allocated half of its 408 garage spaces (serving 1,150 employees) to HOV users, one quarter to vendors and visitors, and one quarter to SOV users. The HOV spaces were reserved and priced at $45 per month for 2-person carpools, and free for carpools of 3 or more. SOV users were charged at a rate equivalent to $60 per month, the same as market rates, but payable daily. Moreover, the SOV parking was available only on a first come-first served basis, making SOV parking availability on-site unreliable. Parking at off-site locations at market rates was an option. Additional elements of US WEST's TDM program included flexible work hours and an on-site transportation coordinator.

Analysis. The vehicle trip making intensity of US WEST and other firms under study was documented from travel surveys that established work trip mode shares for employees of the individual companies. The "vehicle trip rate" was computed as the ratio of motorized vehicle trips to the movement of people in the travel population, in this case, the employees of US WEST going to and from work in 1988. The measure includes public transportation users and non-motorized travelers (the bicycle and walk modes), and a standardized calculation of vehicle trips per person trip for each individual travel mode. Comparative vehicle trip rates were computed for control sites. In the case of US WEST, these were the remainder of employers in downtown Bellevue.

Results. With the parking pricing and space management program described above, US WEST realized mode shares for its employees of 26 percent drive alone, 45 percent carpool, 2 percent vanpool, and 13 percent transit. An additional 2 percent of employees were classified as other, and 13 percent as multimodal, meaning that they used more than one mode to reach the site, such as driving to carpool or transit. Based on additional information from the city of Bellevue, it appears that most of the trips listed as multimodal were in fact drive alone commuters utilizing an alternative fringe parking site near US WEST and then carpooling to the work site in order to gain the carpool parking privileges. As a worst case scenario, with the multimodal trips assumed to be SOV, the vehicle trip rate for US WEST was calculated to be 0.57 per employee. The trip rate for remaining sites in downtown Bellevue averaged 0.83 per employee, meaning that US WEST's trip rate was about 31 percent below ambient levels.

More... It is reported that many US WEST employees were initially somewhat bitter about the need to find alternative travel arrangements when the company relocated to Bellevue, but soon adapted, aided by their prior experience of commuting into Seattle with heavy use of carpooling and transit.

Sources: Comsis Corporation and Harold Katz and Associates, "Evaluation of Travel Demand Management Measures to Relieve Congestion." Federal Highway Administration, Washington,DC (1990). • Comsis Corporation and Institute of Transportation Engineers, "Implementing Effective Travel Demand Management Measures: Inventory of Measures and Synthesis of Experience." Prepared for Federal Highway Administration and Federal Transit Administration, Washington, DC (1993). • US WEST vehicle trip rate recalculation by Handbook authors.

Contrasting Approaches to Parking Pricing in Downtown Los Angeles

Situation. This study compared two companies in downtown Los Angeles that were occupants of identical 52-story office towers on a site that is well-served by transit. The two towers shared a single subterranean parking facility, in which spaces were available for lease on a monthly basis. Employees of the two companies were also served by a nearby multilevel parking structure.

Actions. Table 13-26 summarizes the range of transportation subsidies provided at the two companies. Company A, occupying 54 percent of the floor area in one of the towers, employed 2,045 workers and had no organized ridesharing program. Company A leased 508 spaces for its employees at $100 per month and then charged the employees using these spaces $60 per month. A waiting list for the subsidized spaces at Company A forced some employees to park at off-site locations, pay the full market rate for parking at the site, or use an alternative mode.

Company B occupied 90 percent of the other office tower and employed 1,200 employees. Company B leased 710 parking spaces, which were offered to SOV users at $50 per month and to two-person carpools at $25 per month. Carpools of three or more received free parking, a subsidy of $100 per vehicle. The greatest parking subsidy per employee thus actually accrued to single drivers. Company B also had a well-developed program to promote HOV and transit use, including a travel allowance for vanpoolers.

Analysis. A short survey was used to collect information on the journey to work for a sample of employees at both companies. The response rate was nearly 100 percent, resulting in a sample of about 5 percent of the workforce of both Companies A and B. Table 13-26 presents the mode shares observed at the two companies.

Results. The costs of the two transportation subsidy programs were compared along with the effects on mode choice. The costs of Company A's program were $9.94 per month per employee, once the cost of subsidizing the 508 spaces was distributed over all 2,045 employees. Company B's costs, taking into account the variable costs per employee by mode, averaged $43.62 per employee per month. Company A's program thus achieved the same level of SOV commuting at a far lower cost per employee than Company B. It is worth noting, however, that Company A's program had a stronger element of parking supply restriction than did Company B's (0.24 versus 0.59 subsidized spaces per employee).

Table 13-26 Parking Cost and Mode Choice at Two Companies in Downtown Los Angeles

	Company A	Company B
Cost per Leased Parking Space	$100.00	$100.00
Monthly Subsidy per Vehicle:		
• Solo Drivers	$40.00	$50.00
• Carpools of Two	$40.00	$75.00
• Carpools of Three	$40.00	$100.00
• Vanpools[a]	$40.00	$250.00[b]
Monthly Subsidy per Employee:		
• Solo Drivers	$40.00	$50.00
• Carpools of Two	$20.00	$37.50
• Carpools of Three	$13.33[c]	$33.33
• Vanpools[a]	$4.00[c]	$25.00
• Public Transit Users	none	$15.00
Other TDM Program Elements	No organized program	Active program
Commute Modes (Survey):		
• Drive Alone	49%	48%
• Carpool/Vanpool	20%	34%
• Transit	31%	18%

Notes: [a] Assumed vanpool occupancy of ten employees per van.

[b] Consists of a $100 parking subsidy plus a $15 travel allowance per employee.

[c] Company A had no rideshare subsidy program. These dollar values are calculated by the Handbook authors assuming the per-vehicle parking subsidy to be shared among vehicle occupants.

Source: Mehranian et al (1987).

More... It is also noteworthy that the transit mode share was substantially higher at Company A, where no differential subsidies to carpool parking were provided. The authors concluded that simple elimination of parking subsidies to solo drivers is the more cost effective strategy if the desired TDM objective is reduced SOV commuting and promotion of transit use.

Source: Mehranian, M., Wachs, M., Shoup, D., and Platkin, R., "Parking Cost and Mode Choices Among Downtown Workers: A Case Study." *Transportation Research Record 1130* (1987).

REFERENCES

Association for Commuter Transportation, "Commute Benefit Programs." ACT Home Web Page, Internet (Webpages accessed June, 1999).

Charles River Associates, Inc., "Madison Peak-Period Parking Pricing Demonstration Project." Urban Mass Transit Administration, Washington, DC (1984).

Comsis Corporation and Harold Katz and Associates, "Evaluation of Travel Demand Management Measures to Relieve Congestion." Federal Highway Administration, Washington, DC (1990).

Comsis Corporation and Institute of Transportation Engineers, "Implementing Effective Travel Demand Management Measures: Inventory of Measures and Synthesis of Experience." Prepared for Federal Highway Administration and Federal Transit Administration, Washington, DC (1993).

Comsis Corporation, "Task 2 Working Paper: An Examination of Cost/Benefit and Other Decision Factors Used in Design of Employer-Based TDM Programs." TCRP Project B-4, Unpublished Research Findings, Transportation Research Board, Washington, DC (1994).

Deakin, E., Harvey, G., Pozdena, R., and Yarema, G., *Transportation Pricing Strategies for California: An Assessment of Congestion, Emissions, Energy and Equity Impacts.* Final Report. Prepared for California Air Resources Board, Sacramento, CA (1996).

Dornan, D., and Keith, R., *Parking Pricing Demonstration in Eugene, Oregon.* Prepared for the Urban Mass Transportation Administration by Peat, Marwick, Mitchell and Company, Washington, DC (1988)

Dowling, R., Feltham, D., and Wycko, W., "Factors Affecting Transportation Demand Management Program Effectiveness at Six San Francisco Medical Institutions." *Transportation Research Record 1321* (1991).

Dueker, K. J., Strathman, J. G., and Bianco, M. J., "Strategies to Attract Auto Users to Public Transportation." *TCRP Report 40*, Transportation Research Board, Washington, DC (1998).

Feeney, B. P., "A Review of the Impact of Parking Policy Measures on Travel Demand." *Transportation Planning and Technology*, Vol. 13 (1989).

Glazer, A., and Niskanen, E., "Parking Fees and Congestion." *Regional Science and Urban Economics*, 22 (1992).

Hensher, D. A., and King, J., "Parking Demand and Responsiveness to Supply, Pricing and Location in the Sydney Central Business District." *Transportation Research Part A 35* (2001).

JHK & Associates and K.T. Analytics, Inc., "Analysis of Indirect Source Trip Activity: Regional Shopping Centers." Phase III Market Research and Transportation Management Services. Prepared for California Air Resources Board, Sacramento, CA (November, 1993).

Kolozsvari, D., and Shoup, D., "Turning Small Change into Big Changes." *Access, No. 23* (Fall, 2003)

K.T. Analytics, Inc., "Parking Cash Out." *TDM Status Report*, Federal Transit Administration, Washington, DC (February, 1994).

Kulash, D., *Parking Taxes as Roadway Prices: A Case Study of the San Francisco Experience.* The Urban Institute, Paper 1212-9, Washington, DC (1974).

Kunze, B., Heramb, C., and Martin, T., "Impacts of Municipal Parking-Fee Increases in Downtown Chicago." *Transportation Research Record 786* (1980).

Kuppam, A., Pendyala, R., and Gollakoti, M., *Analysis of the Potential Effectiveness of Parking Pricing Based Transportation Control Measures Using Stated Response Data.* University of South Florida, Department of Civil and Environmental Engineering, Tampa, FL (1997).

Laube, M., and Dansker, B., *Analysis of Parking Management Strategies for the Boston Region.* CTPS Technical Report 38. Central Transportation Planning Staff, Boston, MA (1983).

Mehranian, M., Wachs, M., Shoup, D., and Platkin, R., "Parking Cost and Mode Choices Among Downtown Workers: A Case Study." *Transportation Research Record 1130* (1987).

Metro and Oregon Department of Transportation, "Traffic Relief Options Study," with Technical Appendix. Portland, OR (November, 2000).

Miller, G. K., and Everett, C. T., "Raising Commuter Parking Prices - An Empirical Study." *Transportation 11* (1982).

Olsson, M., and Miller, G., *Parking Discounts and Carpool Formation in Seattle.* The Urban Institute, Paper 5050-3-8, Washington, DC (1978).

Peat, Marwick, Mitchell & Co., "West University Neighborhood Parking Pricing Demonstration Program in Eugene, Oregon." Final Report, Washington, DC (1985).

Portland State University, "Policy Options to Attract Auto Users to Public Transportation." Volume II: Technical Report (Preliminary Draft Final Report), prepared for the Transit Cooperative Research Program. Portland, OR (December, 1995).

Rutherford, S., Badgett, S., Ishimaro, J., and MacLanchlan, S., "Transportation Demand Management: Case Studies of Medium-Sized Employers." *Transportation Research Record 1459* (1995).

Shoup, D., *The Effects of Employer-Paid Parking in Downtown Los Angeles: A Study of Office Workers and Their Employers.* Southern California Association of Governments, Los Angeles, CA (1990).

Shoup, D. C., *Cashing Out Employer-Paid Parking: An Opportunity to Reduce Minimum Parking Requirements.* University of California Transportation Center Working Paper, Berkeley, CA (1994a).

Shoup, D., "Cashing Out Employer-Paid Parking: A Precedent for Congestion Pricing?" *Curbing Gridlock: Peak-period Fees to Relieve Traffic Congestion, Special Report 242, Vol. 2.* Transportation Research Board, Washington, DC (1994b).

Shoup, D., *Evaluating the Effects of Parking Cash Out: Eight Case Studies.* Final Report. Prepared for California Air Resources Board Research Division, Sacramento, CA (1997).

Urban Transportation Monitor, "This Week's Survey Results – CBD Parking." Vol. 7, No. 6 (April 2, 1993).

Valk, P., Transportation Management Services. Chapter 13 review notes (May, 1999).

Victoria Transport Policy Institute, "Online TDM Encyclopedia." http://www.vtpi.org/tdm/ (Website updated December 17, 2003).

HOW TO ORDER *TCRP REPORT 95*

Ch. 1 – Introduction (2005)

Multimodal/Intermodal Facilities

Ch. 2 – HOV Facilities (2005)

Ch. 3 – Park-and-Ride and Park-and-Pool (2004)

Transit Facilities and Services

Ch. 4 – Busways, BRT and Express Bus (2005)

Ch. 5 – Vanpools and Buspools (2005)

Ch. 6 – Demand Responsive/ADA (2004)

Ch. 7 – Light Rail Transit (2005)

Ch. 8 – Commuter Rail (2005)

Public Transit Operations

Ch. 9 – Transit Scheduling and Frequency (2004)

Ch. 10 – Bus Routing and Coverage (2004)

Ch. 11 – Transit Information and Promotion (2003)

Transportation Pricing

Ch. 12 – Transit Pricing and Fares (2004)

Ch. 13 – Parking Pricing and Fees (2005)

Ch. 14 – Road Value Pricing (2003)

Land Use and Non-Motorized Travel

Ch. 15 – Land Use and Site Design (2003)

Ch. 16 – Pedestrian and Bicycle Facilities (2005)

Ch. 17 – Transit Oriented Design (2005)

Transportation Demand Management

Ch. 18 – Parking Management and Supply (2003)

Ch. 19 – Employer and Institutional TDM Strategies (2005)

TCRP Report 95 chapters will be published as stand-alone volumes. Estimated publication dates are in parentheses. Each chapter may be ordered for $20.00. *Note:* Only those chapters that have been released will be available for order.

To order *TCRP Report 95* on the Internet, use the following address:

www.trb.org/trb/bookstore/

At the prompt, type in TC095 and then follow the online instructions. Payment must be made using VISA, MasterCard, or American Express.